FEMALE DESIRES

FEMALE DESIRES

How They Are Sought, Bought and Packaged

Rosalind Coward

GROVE PRESS, INC./New York

First published in 1984 by
PALADIN BOOKS
London

First Grove Press Edition 1985
First Printing 1985
ISBN: 0-394-54591-5
Library of Congress Catalog Card Number: 84-73207

First Evergreen Edition 1985
First Printing 1985
ISBN: 0-394-62367-3
Library of Congress Catalog Card Number: 84-73207

Library of Congress Cataloging in Publication Data
Coward, Rosalind.
   Female desires.

   British ed. published under title: Female desire.
   Bibliography: p.
   1. Women—Psychology—Addresses, essays, lectures.
2. Women—Sexual behavior—Addresses, essays, lectures.
3. Pleasure—Addresses, essays, lectures. 4. Desire—
Addresses, essays, lectures. 5. Femininity (Psychology)
—Addresses, essays, lectures. I. Title.
HQ1206.C725   1985   155.3 '33   84-73207
ISBN 0-394-54591-5
ISBN 0-394-62367-3 (1st Evergreen ed.: pbk.)

Printed in the United States of America

GROVE PRESS, INC., 196 West Houston Street, New York, N.Y. 10014

1   3   5   4   2

THIS BOOK IS DEDICATED
TO THE MEMORY OF SUE CARTLEDGE

Contents

Contents

PART IV: THE STORY

PART V: THE INSTINCT

Acknowledgments

I am extremely grateful to the following people who gave me very helpful comments on all or parts of this book: Judy Holder, Pam Taylor, Wendy Clark, Ann Wickham, Sue Lawrence, Margaret Page, Fran Bennett, Barbara Taylor, and my sister Hilary Webb. I am especially grateful to Maria Black, Ann McAllister and John Ellis for their extensive help with the book.

I am grateful to my parents for help, and especially my mother, Kathleen Sybil Coward, for collecting material over the past few years. I would also like to acknowledge the following people who either discussed some of the ideas or provided material for the book: Sheelagh Sheean, Sarah Montgomery, Karen Alexander, Christine Pearce, Tessa Adams, Mary Massey, Anne Karpf, Jo Spence, Chris Wilson, Peter Lewis, Stuart Hood and Peter Meyer.

Thanks to Diana Cooke for her help with the typing. And especial thanks to Bette Chapkis for doing the picture research.

I am also indebted to Litza Jansz for providing the cartoons for this book; to Mitra Tabrizian for permission to reproduce her photograph as illustration for the chapter 'Being Fashionable'; and to James Swinson for permission to reproduce his photograph for 'Men's Bodies'; thanks also to: Bantam Books Inc; Richardson-Vicks Ltd and Roche Products Ltd; The National Magazine Company and the Hillelson Agency for the photograph of Ornella Muti by Greg Gorman of Sygma; Euroflair; Dance Centre; National Dairy Council; Kobal Collection; Milk Marketing Board and Ogilvy and Mather; Ashe Laboratories Ltd and Saatchi and Saatchi Garland-Compton Ltd; Syndication International Ltd and Mrs Marjorie Proops; Ardea, Arthur Bertrand and Alan Wearing.

A version of 'Naughty But Nice: Food Pornography' first appeared in the *Guardian*.

Introduction

Female Desire is a collection of essays about pleasure: about things women enjoy; about things women are said to enjoy; and about things women are meant to enjoy and don't.

These essays follow the lure of pleasure across a multitude of different cultural phenomena, from food to family snapshots, from royalty to nature programmes. Everywhere women are offered pleasure. Pleasure if we lose weight, pleasure if we prepare a beautiful meal, pleasure if we follow a natural instinct, pleasure if we acquire something new – a new body, a new house, a new outfit, a new relationship.

Pleasure is this society's permanent Special Offer. But some drive is needed to take up that offer. And it is female desire which makes us respond, and take up the offer.

To be a woman is to be constantly addressed, to be constantly scrutinized, to have our desire constantly courted – in the kitchen, on the streets, in the world of fashion, in films and fiction. Issuing forth from books and magazines, from films and television, from the radio, there are endless questions about what women desire, endless theories and opinions are offered. Desire is endlessly defined and stimulated. Everywhere, female desire is sought, bought, packaged and consumed.

Female desire is courted with the promise of future perfection, by the lure of achieving ideals – ideal legs, ideal hair, ideal homes, ideal sponge cakes, ideal relationships. The ideals on offer don't actually exist except as the end product of photographic techniques or as elaborate fantasies. But these ideals are held out to women – all the time. Things may be bad, life may be difficult, relationships may be unsatisfying, you may be feeling unfulfilled, but there's always promise of improvement. Achieve these ideals and you will feel better! Female dissatisfaction is constantly recast as desire, as desire for something more, as the perfect reworking of what has already gone before – dissatisfaction displaced into desire for the ideal.

Our desire sustains us, but it also sustains a way of living which may not ultimately be the best and only way for women. Women shopping, cooking, buying and wearing the goods produced by this society; women marrying, taking the responsibility for children, nurturing others; women decorating and displaying homes – all these practices are sustained by female desire. The pleasure/desire axis sustains social forms which keep things as they are. The

pleasure/desire axis appears to be everything women want but it
may involve loss – loss of opportunity, loss of freedom, perhaps even
loss of happiness.

Female desire is crucial to our whole social structure. Small
wonder it is so closely observed, so endlessly pursued, so frequently
recast and reformulated.

Female Desire attempts to get inside the offer of pleasure and the
game of desire. But in analysing these pleasures, these essays are not
denying pleasure. This society tends to treat pleasure as sacrosanct.
Those who examine it are seen as killjoys, against life, against
nature. But pleasures, like everything else, change. Pig-sticking isn't
so popular now; nor is bear-baiting. But there was a time when they
were as popular as 'Coronation Street'. Pleasure isn't an eternal
emotion, above history or critical investigation. Pleasure can be
created, and stage-managed. And perhaps the pleasures offered to
women now may be tying women to structures which in the end are
destructive of joy, if indulgent of pleasure.

But there's another emotion which comes with pleasure, like a
faithful old dog that won't be shaken off. Guilt. Women know all
about guilt – it's our speciality. Pleasure generates guilt, and that's
bad enough. But even worse is the guilt that is generated when other
people discuss our pleasures critically – guilt if we enjoy cooking,
guilt if we like clothes, guilt if we go on a diet. Even as a feminist
I've felt that sinking feeling of 'I shouldn't be doing this'. Not
because anyone has told me I shouldn't be doing this, but because I
know such practices have been analysed and criticized. Guilt in fact
has been the habitual reaction of many women to feminism – guilt at
liking conventionally feminine things, guilt about being married,
guilt about wanting to stay at home with children. Pleasure may be
sacrosanct but guilt is remorseless.

In *Female Desire* I'm not approaching 'feminine' pleasures as an
outsider; nor as a stranger to guilt. The pleasures I describe are
often my pleasures. Food, cooking, clothes, novels, soap operas,
houses, nature programmes – these are all my enjoyments. I don't
approach these things as a distant critic but as someone examining
myself, examining my own life under a microscope. But nor will I
treat these pleasures as sacrosanct. Good girls enjoy what they're
given but what they're given may not always be good for them.

This book has not been written as a result of painstaking
academic research on each of the topics, although it is informed by
previous theoretical studies of these issues. My fieldwork has been

on myself and on my friends and family, whom I have submitted to incessant interrogation about their private lives, their hopes and dreams. Quite deliberately these essays aim at no more than understanding how the representations directed at women enmesh with our actual lives. What are these representations? How do they relate to the reality of women's lives? And how much of a solution would it be to pursue the forms of pleasure presumed to be women's pleasures?

Even while writing this book, while submitting these representations to critical scrutiny, still the representations didn't always lose their hold. I took my body in hand seriously at least five times during these months. The healthy life lasted about three days in each case, after which I was back to my old degenerate ways. After all, I consoled myself, I was working very hard. I also moved house, fantasized about doing it up and then watched with alarm my discontent travel from room to room like a home-owner's hypochondria. I read a lot of novels, watched a lot of films, and fantasized a lot. I worried about relationships and family, talked about them to whoever would listen, and consumed all available literature on the subject. In short I responded like many women to the definitions of female desire held out to me and the lure of pleasure offered.

But there were other things as well, a lot of things in my life – as in the lives of all women – which just weren't catered for in the mass of representations aimed at female desire. There was love between friends; there was the death of a friend and loss; there were confused feelings about sexual identity; and there was anger at the ways in which women are treated. There was work at an institution where I felt undervalued by male management. And there was anger at the responsibilities which women all around me were shouldering, responsibilities for the future, responsibilities for communication, responsibilities for the caring side of society – all undervalued and trivialized by the representation of female desire offered by our male-dominated society.

In the end, the excess of *these* feelings outweighed the other promises held out to me. In the end I was not convinced that the pleasures offered, the promises made, or the definitions given were adequate. So many of the promises tell us that women can improve their lives without any major social changes. I don't believe that. The pleasures offered, the solutions held out, neither exhaust what there is to be said about female desire, nor do they actually offer any solution. Subtly, in complicated ways, recognizing some conflict and problems, discourses on female desire nevertheless work inexorably towards closure, towards putting the lid on love, desire and especially on change.

The aim of *Female Desire* is to examine how presumptions about female pleasure and female desire are shot through so many cultural practices, and to look at the way our desire is courted even in our most everyday experiences as women. I don't treat these cultural representations as the forcible imposition of false and limiting stereotypes. Instead I explore the desire presumed by these representations, the desire which touches feminist and non-feminist women alike. But nor do I treat female desire as something universal, unchangeable, arising from the female condition. I see the representations of female pleasure and desire as *producing* and sustaining feminine positions. These positions are neither distant roles imposed on us from outside which it would be easy to kick off, nor are they the essential attributes of femininity. Feminine positions are produced as responses to the pleasures offered to us; our subjectivity and identity are formed in the definitions of desire which encircle us. These are the experiences which make change such a difficult and daunting task, for female desire is constantly lured by discourses which sustain male privilege.

These essays are about the feelings which sustain, endorse or reject the definitions of female desire offered to us. And they are about the contradictions, the elements which don't fit together, about the information omitted, and about the precariousness of the representations. Above all these essays listen out for the pleasures which escape, slip out between the cracks and perhaps spell the ruin of existing definitions of female desire.

PART 1

THE
LOOK

Feel Good, Look Great!

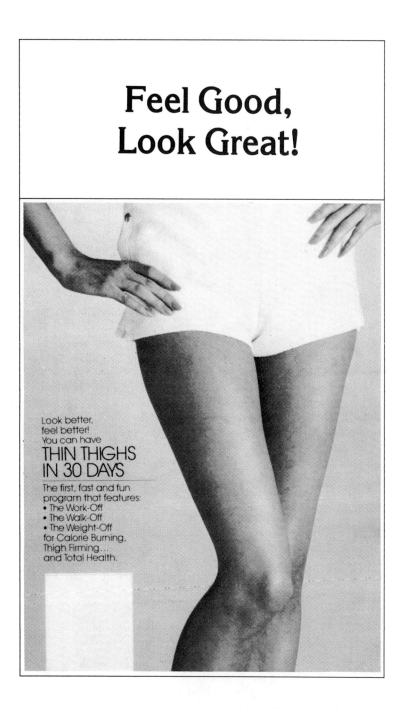

Look better,
feel better!
You can have
THIN THIGHS
IN 30 DAYS

The first, fast and fun
program that features:
• The Work-Off
• The Walk-Off
• The Weight-Off
for Calorie Burning,
Thigh Firming...
and Total Health.

'Attitude', says the first entry in a health and beauty A–Z, is 'as good a place as any to begin. Because no creams or lotions or lists of information are going to make as big an impact on the way you look and feel as your attitude to your body' (*Honey A–Z of Your Body*).

Feeling good about your body is big in health and beauty circles at the moment. In fact, the way health has been equated with beauty over the past few years is witness to the shift in emphasis. Gone are the days when women were exhorted to violent and 'faddish' diets which would miraculously transform their appearance. Now 'health and beauty' features in magazines, on chat shows and radio programmes are all dominated by a call to overall fitness. The art of body maintenance has been truly established. While this ideology of health and fitness has clearly affected men and women of all ages, it has nevertheless been directed at women in a particular way, enmeshing with other very definite attitudes towards the body and appearance.

On the surface, this concern with feeling good appears to be a healthy corrective to the earlier obsessions with violent diets and their ultimate aim of 'losing ten pounds in a fortnight'. Instead we are encouraged to remember the integration of body and mind and to consider the psychological aspects of the body's well-being. Now there is a belief 'that we're not just body but mind and spirit as well. All three are interlinked and must be healthy' ('The Body Boom', *Cosmopolitan*, August 1982).

In part, this new emphasis is a response to the pressure mounted by feminists against the crude and dangerous ideology of the instant diet. Women like Susie Orbach in *Fat is a Feminist Issue* argued that women's relationships with their eating habits and their body shape are complicated psychological issues. Crash diets, diet plans and diet aids only contributed to women's already tortuous and guilty relationship with eating. What's more, they rarely worked and were potentially dangerous, sometimes making women seriously ill.

But the new emphasis on overall health is only in part a response to these kinds of criticisms. Because it is also a new kind of obsession, which has the effect of making the female body a particular site of concern for Western culture. This new obsession makes women the bearers of a whole series of preoccupations about sex and health. For the exhortations to good health are exhortations to take control of your life, and are in no way separate from ideologies of working at becoming sexually attractive.

The messages are clear. You must eat healthily: 'It's no secret that eating properly is the key to mental and physical balance. Unless you eat healthily, no exercise in the world will make you lose weight' (*Woman's Own*, July 1982). Eating well will improve your looks. For example, you can follow a 'Clear Skin Diet' which 'is full of all the requisite tissue-building nutrients to help your skin look and feel its best ever'. If you 'follow the clear skin diet for one week' you will see how your skin responds with *'glowing good health'* (*Cosmopolitan*, November 1980). In addition, eating the right foods will make you feel better; you'll have more energy. A doctor (in *Annabel*) recommends a change to a high-fruit, high-cereal diet. Why? Because they are 'very energy dilute'. In addition to the change to high-energy foods, there is exercise. More than anything else, physical exercise is offered as the activity which will guarantee the healthier body. Go dancing, swimming, go jogging or pursue a physical fitness routine as punishing as that devised by Jane Fonda. To take your body in hand in this way will reap unexpected rewards. Instead of feeling totally burnt out as you might expect, you will find yourself abounding with energy; you will have speeded up your metabolism. The words encountered over and over again are 'invigorated', 'energized', 'enthusiastic'.

Mental energy, then, is at the heart of these discourses. The *loss* of ten pounds in a fortnight may be beyond the capabilities of the average woman, but the *acquisition* of new attitudes is certainly not. Revitalization, it seems, is within the easy grasp of us all and enables us to come to terms with the fact that we are not exactly like the models. A mood of mock self-depreciation has spread over beauty writing, as if there were a conspiracy among the less fortunate: 'Tall, slim, beautiful, witty, energetic, a talented designer with her own business, an excellent cook . . . Damn it, there must be something wrong with her – ingrown toe-nails, split ends, fat ankles?' (*Options*, August 1982). But this conspiratorial tone is directed towards an end; we *can* do something about ourselves. We can change our attitude by doing some work on our bodies.

A beauty correspondent on the radio recently gave an outline for a typical schedule for this body-work. She outlined a week-end schedule of 'beauty care' which involved eating high-energy food, going out jogging, exercising at home, and 'aquatherapy' (lying in the bath squeezing the flab). The promised outcome? 'You'll feel super *and* have lost three pounds in weight.'

And here's the rub. As they affect women, these ideas about

health always end up around the question of appearance. Feel better and you'll look better.

> Exercise, is, of course, essential. And there's no excuse for not doing some. It improves circulation and oxygen flow. It tones up floppy muscles, speeds up your metabolism, burns off calories. It relieves nervous tension. It keeps you supple and lithe and stops joints stiffening up as you age. And it makes you feel healthy, invigorated, alive; which in turn makes you *look* it.
>
> *Honey A–Z of Your Body*

The emphasis on the right mental attitude and the route to good health are subordinated to an overall requirement: their end product is that we should look better. Even those articles and programmes that have picked up on feminism's critique of the coercive power of the ideal shape are invariably accompanied by glossy pictures of models conforming to the ideal we are supposed to forget. They promote a paradoxical attitude. If you forget about wanting to conform to the ideal and relax, concentrate on your overall well-being, you will all the more easily reach that ideal. The concern with visible appearance has hegemonized any real understanding of health and the integration of mental and physical well-being. Above all, good mental and physical health will bear the fruits of a better appearance; they will give us the energy to do something about our shape.

A recent article entitled 'How I thought myself thin' represents clearly the drift of the ideology. Here *Fat is a Feminist Issue* has been picked up as another diet aid, a phenomenon doubtless promoted by the English publisher's insistence (against the author's wishes) that it should be subtitled 'How to lose weight permanently without dieting'.

> I came to look on losing weight as an educational exercise. Learning not just in the theoretical sense, but in an absolutely real way how much I could eat without gaining weight. It was absorbing in an almost scientific sense. And what kept me going week after week was exploring the fascinating mental attitudes which had made me fat in the first place. These amounted to self-deception, laziness about all the sort of opting-out that Susie Orbach writes about.
>
> 'How I thought myself thin', *Cosmopolitan*, August 1982

What this emphasis on the mind controlling the body has done is in some ways worse than the ideology that preceded it. The old ideas told us our bodies weren't in good shape. But at least we could blame that on nature, if even dieting didn't get rid of 'cellulite jodhpurs'. But now our minds are the problem. We could think ourselves thin, if only we had the will-power to change our lifestyle and generate the energy necessary to exercise to 'get really fit and dramatically change the shape of your body' (*Honey A–Z of Your Body*).

> Have you ever envied models and actresses their slim and supple bodies and glowing good looks? Have you ever thought I could never have a body like that, because . . . and reached for another chocolate biscuit in the same breath? Do you recognise any of these excuses? – Big Bones – No will-power – Husband likes me cute and cuddly. Well, no more excuses! You *can* have a beautiful body if you really want one. After all, it's your body in the first place – and it's your responsibility to take good care of it. All you need is a little know-how and some will-power.
>
> 'Look Great, Feel Better', *Annabel*, December 1980

Vigorous exercise, it seems, can solve all our problems. The instructions are not clear on what to do if you don't have the energy to crawl out of bed in the morning . . .

Several promises, then, constitute the lure of this feel-good ideology. First, that it is the ultimately efficient way of dramatically changing your body shape. And it goes without saying that the change will be in the direction of the cultural ideal discussed in 'The Body Beautiful' (see Page 37). Secondly, it's a way of achieving this shape (or remaining fashionably slim as they say) while *consuming more*. This may appear paradoxical given that there is still the preoccupation with losing weight, with dieting, with concentrating obsessively on what you eat. Nevertheless, it's clear from expressions and words used that a flush of expansionism has spread over the contracting body. Change the metabolic rate and, above all, burn off more calories; the incitements to *eat more efficiently* are equally incitements to eat more. The much heralded F-Plan diet seems to be a well-received solution. A diet without dieting, where more fibre will help the body shed those extra pounds.

Finally, these ideas express a concern with women's well-being, but reduce it to these pseudo-medical preoccupations with figure, fitness and firmness. Fatigue, weariness, lethargy – which are in fact the deadening symptoms of depression or general ill health – are all potentially 'cured' by taking your body in hand. Even Jill Tweedie, a writer usually highly critical of media stereotypes, seems to have dabbled in this ideology. In the article entitled 'Now when I glimpse depression I have tricks to forestall it' (*Cosmopolitan*, August 1982) she writes:

> I also attend to my body, something I once thought far too undramatic and suburban a thing to do. My soul in upheaval and you talk of a tonic or Vitamin C? Cold showers? Walks around the block? Would anyone have dared suggest that cure to Byron? Still the links between the body and the mind are indissoluble and the banal fact is that forcing oxygen down the lungs does, sometimes, set the mood afloat again.

I am not trying to cast doubt on the fact that good health, exercise, fresh air and good food are preconditions for feeling well. Instead, I am trying to pinpoint the way that these are offered up to women in a very particular way as solutions to illness and depression. These solutions are invariably tangled up with the narcissistic construction of women as objects for 'the look' which may itself be a factor in causing women's depression.

Depression has only recently become a matter which can be discussed in terms that are not exclusively those of the medical and the psychiatric. Within medicine, the dominant explanation of depression has been expressed in terms of physical and chemical disposition. The preferred treatment of depression has often been intervention around the body: drugs, shock treatment, and so on. Even though psychoanalysis and psychotherapy are recognized as valid, indeed significant forms of response to depression, they nevertheless remain marginal to the medical institutions, although always available with private finance. But recently depression has been recognized as requiring sociological explanations as well. And what has been revealed by such enquiries is the far greater incidence of depression among women.

This has not been in any way surprising to those who are aware that the objective conditions of women's lives are on the whole more difficult than those of men. But even though it is recognized that illness and depression may have social causes, discourses on health and beauty continue to offer this pseudo-medical solution to depression. It is still the individual body where the changes can be effected. Health is presented as something which calls for individual hard work, not social solutions. And the proof that women have done that work is also their reward – the fashionably slim body.

Being Fashionable

The look that launched a thousand snips.

MITRA TABRIZIAN

One thing that fashion is quite categorically *not* is an expression of individuality. By definition, fashion implies a mode of dress, or overall style, which is accepted as representing up-to-dateness. Fashion, of course, is not necessarily the same thing as clothes which are often used in individual ways. Being fashionable is different. It is always the acceptance of the prevailing ideals.

These prevailing ideals change considerably from year to year and most women are not immune to these changes. Fashion is always at least partially perceived, even by women uninterested in the 'annual suicide' of styles or who use their clothes very deliberately to make social or political statements. Our barely perceived, subconscious responses to shifting ideals are always thrown into sharp relief by looking at old photos. 'How on earth could we have worn bell-bottomed trousers and platform heels? Ugh! Don't they look repulsive?' The litmus test of a change is when a style once slavishly followed is viewed with incomprehension and almost revulsion.

A style once willingly adopted becomes a stigma of outmoded ugliness; here is the mechanism of fashion. More than the adoption of the new, it is also the certain death (or at least deep coma) of what has gone before.

'*Did* you see Audrey Hepburn in that old movie on the telly?' exclaimed the woman at the dinner party. 'All those tailored couture clothes hacked off six inches above the knees. *So* out of proportion. So unflattering. How *could* we have thought it looked nice? We must have been mad. I certainly wouldn't *dream* of ever wearing a mini again – whatever you fashion writers may dictate.'

B. Polan, *Guardian*, 10 September 1980

Such dinner-party chatter undoubtedly poured new blood into an old corpse. The mini-skirt rose Dracula-like from its sleep, with a defiant new meaning addressed to the generation who had come to view it with horror.

Fashion's mysterious cycle of death and rebirth, avarice and disgust is pretty well sex-specific; women alone are subject to its curious workings. Yes, men now wear ear-rings, sometimes – though rarely – make-up and have passed through brightly coloured dungarees to the beaten-leather look. But compared to female fashions, men's have changed absolutely minimally. The fundamental outline of the clothes and the fundamental elements have remained constant for a long time now. Hippy robes and long hair in the sixties were the nearest male dress has come to a radical transformation, and these changes touched only a relatively small subgroup.

The elements of men's dress are really very limited. There's a range of possible tops – a jumper, t-shirt, jacket – and trousers of one kind or another. Even boiler suits were just one-piece versions of the same. For men, the statements made with clothes are largely restricted to political or cultural statements: business men, punk, heavy metal. All these cover men's bodies in similar ways, following the outline of the male body.

Women's clothes have touched women's bodies in an almost bewildering variety of ways over the last century. Material clings tightly, then hangs in loose folds; belts hold the waist in, then it disappears altogether under rolls of padding; shoulders are revealed, then backs, then legs. Breasts are emphasized, then denied. One moment movement is restricted with pencil skirts, the next free-flowing skirts or baggy trousers emphasize movement and fluidity. Stiletto heels force us up and make bottoms protrude, then flat 'sensible' shoes come into fashion. None of these coverings, uncoverings, restrictions and freedoms has touched the male outline in the same way.

Women's bodies, and the messages which clothes can add, are the repository of the social definitions of sexuality. Men are neutral. Women are always the defined sex and the gyrations around women's clothing are part of the constant pressure towards display of these definitions.

How is it that the definitions addressed to clothes and women's bodies become women's own language? How is it we come to speak the words that are written on our body?

Let us take the example of what the fashion-writers call 'continental chic', the perennial 'little black dress'. It has the odd status of being a fashion which all its adherents represent as being not a fashion, 'above fashion'. Like all 'styles' it is not exclusively about sex, but also makes other statements about class and power.

A given style creates particular meanings which can be read from it. In the case of 'continental chic', the items of clothing, how they are arranged and worn, the style of the body and hair, are geared to expressions of wealth and sophisticated sexuality. And like many 'styles' of the bourgeoisie, this one too represents itself as 'good dress sense', 'a nose' for style.

This style is much promoted by the so-called top end of fashion design. Here we have a quite self-conscious group of designers, suppliers and consumers who consider themselves to be above the contortions and rush of fashion. It is the regime of clothing that is presented as 'classic' and 'timeless'.

> The shape and detail of her clothes is in the mainstream of fashion but like Jean Muir she manages to make them timeless as well – because they bear a signature which is stronger than mere fashion. Like the great Muir, she says: 'I'm not terribly interested in fashion. I just want to make beautiful clothes women will want to wear and wear.'
>
> *Guardian*, 11 February 1981

Fashion-writing everywhere preserves this mystique. The 'truly fashionable' are above fashion:

> St Laurent thinks that a woman, like a man, should be able to possess a wardrobe of clothes that will not date and when I suggested that he couldn't have much of a feel for fashion as such he retorted vehemently, 'I hate fashion.'
>
> *Cosmopolitan*, February 1977

Thus even the fashion-designers whose living is made precisely through the construction of new standards perpetuate this mystique that some clothes and some designs are simply classically elegant, timelessly beautiful.

In fact the regime of clothing and the particular style designated as timelessly glamorous is merely another statement made with clothes, yet it demands a meaning in addition to that of mass-produced fashion, a meaning that it is above the vicissitudes of mass taste. The aim of this style is primarily to connote wealth, through the ideas of elegance and sophistication of tastes. Design is geared to emphasize the texture of the material and the tailoring rather than to emphasize some other 'concept' like hi-tech. So-called simple or conservative styles in jumpers emphasize softness of wool, closeness to the body, the ability to wear such material next to the skin (as with all the expensive fabrics like silk and suede). Jackets and coats emphasize the slender shape of the body, and are cut to follow the shape of the body cleverly. Clothes like jackets or skirts are often lined and linings are opulent and silky. These clothes are designed to make a statement about what they feel like. They are designed to connote a sophisticated sensuality, that enjoys touching itself all the time. 'Sleeping between cool pure linen sheets with a feather-light blanket. The pure silk nightdress costs £185 from Courtnay' ('First Class Return to Romance', *Sunday Times* fashion feature).

These clothes are designed to suggest individual tailoring (even if they aren't individually tailored), expensive fabric, but above all a sensual pleasure in having the body touched. By the suggestion of soft extravagant material, these clothes are intended to suggest a 'sophisticated' sexuality, the sort of sensuality which is meant to come with wealth. It is the sort of sensuality which is supposed to wear silk knickers, sleep in silk sheets, and can afford to spend fortunes on linings just so that the clothes feel nice. Born in Hollywood, and kept alive in the art cinema of Rohmer, it is a clichéed and outmoded sensuality which tries to convince us that the wealthy tastes and practices are the most pleasurable.

'I think there is a tremendous eroticism in the fact that you knew how much somebody paid for a dress,' she purred. 'And Garbo's attitude was terribly sexy when she insisted on wearing silk underwear in her films because she would *know* and *feel* it although nobody else did.'
 Lady Windlesham interviewed in the *Daily Express*, 6 October 1982

This is the secret of such dress. By plain style and soft skin-substitute material it attempts to suggest, paradoxically by its visibility, the invisible, the sensual life of luxury.

The connotations of this style as classic and above fashion are maintained by the fashion industry – one definite style which remains relatively unchanging and the other ('real fashion') submitting itself to the convolutions of annual changes. It reminds me of the educational system in Britain where children are streamed into grades of intelligence (achievers and under-achievers). Yet in an economy which depends on unskilled cheap labour, this streaming is profoundly mystifying. For it presents intelligence and stupidity as God-given attributes when really these categories are required by this particular system; they are merely two types geared towards two different futures. So the fashion industry sets up a realm of 'classic' dress in which meanings of upper-class sexuality can only be maintained while the rest of fashion is rocked by change after change.

But if the less wealthy of us respond to different criteria of fashionableness, we can still learn from the way in which this style creates its meanings. This style aims to suggest an upper-class stereotype of sensuality – leisured, indulgent and self-regarding. Other fashions arise from similar needs to make statements about

sexual inclination (or character), or social and political statements –
how the clothes will be combined with each other, how they will
touch the body, what relationship they have to other clothing
systems which have gone before or coexist beside it.

It is certainly the case that clothing for women has exploded into a
plethora of styles; the trim secretary coexists beside definite feminist
styles. And there are a multitude of pop-group affiliation styles,
statements about what type of music you like, what social events,
styles of behaviour. But in spite of this bewildering configuration,
there are still general overall trends in the realm of fashion. Even if
individuals don't accept a whole outfit, the subconsciously perceived
shifts about shape or length of clothing, which parts to be exposed
and so on, do touch most women. And these changes, no less than
the *idée fixe* of the classic style, represent statements about sexuality.

Changes in style don't simply come from a conspiratorial and
calculating fashion industry determined to make us consume more
and more. The fashion industry (shops, designers, models, advertising) survives on rapid changes but these changes don't necessarily
come from the industry itself. On some occasions where a particular
style has been promoted, it has failed dismally. Values often come
from the use of clothing in subcultures – ear-rings copied from gay
signals, pastiches of fashion from the street parodies of punk. Take
also the series of Third World styles which have passed through the
West: ethnic Indian; Ali-Baba pants and slippers; PLO guerrilla.
All these styles have plundered Third World clothes production,
making extravagant use of sources of cheap (i.e. exploited) labour.
And fashion-writing has obsessively promoted this exotic theme
with clothing, a promotion perhaps not unconnected with photographic sessions in the Bahamas and the Far East which have
become standard perks of the industry.

There are then a number of possible routes leading to the espousal
of one type of material or any one design. The overall style is decided
by how the elements are combined together and what these combinations mean.

Would it be correct, then, to assume that the only way to
understand fashion is to analyse minutely each particular style, to
break down, as with classic style, an endless theatre of different
statements? Do the rapid changes in clothing style throughout the
seventies, say, merely reveal the particular wearer's subgroup
affiliation, with its values of whom to attract, whom to repel, whom
to signal to? Or can we say something about how most women are

susceptible at some general level to changing criteria of attractiveness?

I believe there are general pressures towards 'being fashionable' above and beyond particular subgroup statements. The meaning of this general level of fashionability changes. In the last century, for example, the term 'a lady of fashion' might have signified 'wealthy'. To be fashionable now is, I think, to express a readiness to keep up with prevailing sexual ideals.

Over the last decade, the fashion for women to espouse a variety of men's clothing has provided an interesting example of the way that the idea of fashion works. First there was army gear, then dungarees and boiler suits, followed by more unisex sporty clothes – track suits and jodhpurs, more recently dress suits, and then thirties gangster styles.

Undoubtedly these are powerful signifiers of freedom of movement, meanings of work (dungarees etc.) or freedom of the street (gangsters). The clothing represents an attempt to reclaim the street and work for women. But other elements are combined with these fashions to add other significations. There have been unlikely bedfellows such as jodhpurs and stiletto heels, the latter the ultimate symbol of female oppression and restriction. And equal to the tendency to signify street life has been the transformation of these clothes into their nursery equivalent. For fast behind dungarees came a wave of play clothes: brightly coloured extravaganzas, silver socks, babygros, baggy-bottomed clown trousers, reminiscent in shape of the child in nappies. And more recently the mini-skirt has evoked the rebellious adolescent, hole in tights, refusing to comb her hair. 'Fun' material too has been present – lurex, bright cottons, silver thread, even paper and plastics.

More than any value of sexual ambiguity, or street ideals, or playful subversion of fashionableness, this cross-dressing has been espoused by the fashion industry because it signifies daring. If we have passed through periods of backless fronts, off-the-shoulders, topless bottoms, mini-skirts, the fashion industry has currently moved to overdress. Mock Samurai outfits with huge padded parts, tight belts and uneven hemlines are the apotheosis of this injunction towards daring: the question it asks is, can you get away with it, can you wear something male and ungainly and still look attractive? Being fashionable now is about wearing the bizarre, something which a recent advertising campaign made explicit. *19* magazine offered itself with the image of a model dressed rather like the scarecrow, Worzel Gummidge, with the caption 'Some girls wouldn't dare'. The essence of fashionableness currently is to dare to wear the extraordinary, to look as if you don't care and still remain attractive. The tendency to clutter the body is all part of this. Layers and layers, padding, leather, three belts; what they emphasize is: the wearer's body is good enough for her not to worry.

What might have been a parody or rejection of fashion reveals itself to be well within the tradition of clothes geared towards prevailing standard ideals about female sexual behaviour. Here is the boring legacy of the sixties, the signification of the modern girl who will dare everything (and because of that attract her man).

Nowhere is this clearer than in the adoption of male suits with ties and braces. Some have suggested that this is fashion appropriating meanings which originally came from lesbianism. For from the turn of the century, the adoption of male dress and 'masculine appearance' (cropped hair etc.) was adopted as a sign in the lesbian subculture. It was a means for lesbians simultaneously to disassociate themselves from feminine stereotypes and thereby claim an active sexual identity and a means of recognition. These meanings cannot be totally suppressed even though the style is now high fashion. Nor is there any desire to suppress such meanings. For as it has appeared in high fashion, the slight suggestion of lesbianism is taken as an extreme point of daring. Not that the connotations as they appear in fashion have anything to do with *daring* to love the same sex and all the real daring which the early lesbians lived out. Instead, they have everything to do with *daring* for the attention of men: '[Young women] have gone straight to the source and are shopping for men's wear. *And there's nothing perverse about it at all.* "Men's clothes tend to be cheaper, better made"' *Daily Telegraph*; my emphasis.

This fashionable look – the overbig, often ill-fitting suit and tie – is a statement about daring not to seek the approval of men but presenting yourself in a way so that you know you'll get it. I don't have to seek after male approval (but I'm damn sure I'll get it, because men like women who'll do anything). It is yet again part of the appearance of an ideology which reinforces women's passivity. Women will get a sexual response whether they go looking for it or not.

Fashion is not the forcible imposition of restricting and unsuitable clothing. Being fashionable from the point of view of the fashion industry is merely about the creation of new and daring images, the creation of a sense of the extraordinary. Often the industry is far from being the creator of these new styles and new ways of being daring. It sometimes follows behind the subgroups. But where the fashion industry cannot fail to win is that the extraordinary has always to be renewed, if the signals of sexual adventure are to be continuously communicated.

This constant generation of the new renders previous styles ugly or repellent. They come to signify a *passé* form of behaviour, an outmoded personal behaviour as a defunct style. To see someone dressed in the style of the sixties is to be confronted with someone who just hasn't kept up with the times, who is, in short, a sexual conservative.

The Body
Beautiful

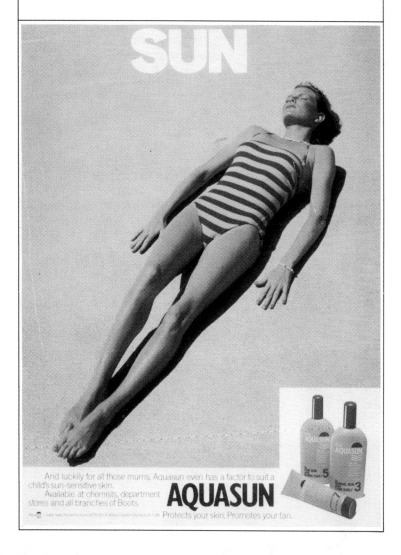

The essence of fashion is that it represents an almost annual – but usually subconsciously perceived shift in what is deemed to look good. Colour, length and shape of clothing have all changed drastically from year to year over the last few decades. What is more, there have been considerable changes in the type of woman whose beauty is taken as exemplary – the difference, for example, between Twiggy or Julie Christie in the sixties, Maria Schneider in the seventies and Nastassia Kinsky in the eighties. But this diversity of colouring, hairstyles, and dress styles disguises what has been a consistent trend in fashion for the last thirty years. The images which have bombarded us over these years leave little doubt that there is one very definite ideal, the ideal of the perfect body.

This is the one fundamental point of agreement in fashion, advertising and glamour photography; the rules are rigid and the contours agreed. There is a definite female outline which is considered the cultural ideal. This 'perfect' female body would be between five foot five and five foot eight, long-legged, tanned and vigorous looking, but above all, without a spare inch of flesh. 'Brown, slim, lively and lovely . . . that's how we would all like to see ourselves on holiday. Here are a few tips on achieving this and maintaining it' (*Ideal Home*).

Ever since the sixties, with its key image of Twiggy, there has been a tendency within fashion- and beauty-writing and imagery towards the idealization of a female body with no fat on it all. Concern with achieving this 'fashionable slimness' has become a routine part of many women's lives; dieting, watching what you eat, feeling guilty about food, and exercising affect most women to a greater or lesser degree.

The ideal outline is the silhouette which is left behind after the abolition of those areas of the body which fashion-writing designates 'problem areas'. First, bottoms:

Female behinds – whether sexy and shapely or absolutely enormous – have long been the subject of saucy seaside postcards. But this important structure can make or mar flimsy summer clothes . . . to say nothing of beachwear. If what goes on below your back is no joke to you, join Norma Knox as she looks at ways to smooth down, gently reshape and generally improve the area between your waist and your knees.

Woman's Own, 24 July 1982

We are encouraged to 'beat saddle-bag hips' because pear-shaped buttocks tend to wear badly in middle age if they have lacked exercise or have been constantly flattened in over-tight trousers' (ibid.). Next we learn of the disadvantages of flabby thighs. We are told to 'ride a bike and firm up *slack* calves and *floppy* thighs'. Elsewhere we learn of the horrors of loose stomach muscles and their dire consequence, 'the pot belly'. Bosoms are a little more recalcitrant but even these can be 'toned up' which means 'your bust's firmness can be improved if the circulation is encouraged' (*Annabel*, December 1980). Finally we should 'Take a Long Look at Legs' (*Woman's Own*, 1 May 1982). The 'best' are 'smooth, flawless, unflabby, and golden'. But there is good news, because 'legs are leaner . . . thanks to dieting and exercise' (ibid.).

And if all or any of these problem parts continue to cause you trouble, you can always resort to the knife – cosmetic surgery. Women's magazines, beauty books and beauty advice regularly give out information about this or make it the subject of light-hearted asides: 'The only known way to remove surplus body fat (short of an operation!) is to consume fewer calories' (John Yudkin). Cosmetic surgery is offered not just for altering the shape of your nose but for cutting away bits of flesh that cling stubbornly to those problem areas.

These exhortations leave us in little doubt that the West has as constricting an ideal of female beauty and behaviour as exists in some non-European societies where clitoridectomy is practised. In the West, the ideal of sexual attractiveness is said to be upheld voluntarily, rather than inflicted by a compulsory operation to change the shape of women's anatomy. But the obsession with one particular shape, everywhere promoted by the media, is no less of a definite statement about expectations for women and their sexuality.

Confronted with the strictness of this cultural ideal, we need to understand the meanings and values attached to this shape. We also need to understand the mechanisms which engage women in a discourse so problematic for us; and we need to know how women actually perceive themselves in relation to this idealized image.

What are the values which Western society attributes to this body shape?

The shape is slim, lacking in 'excess fat' which is defined as any flesh which appears not to be muscled and firm, any flesh where you can 'pinch an inch', as a current slimming dictum suggests. The only area where flesh is tolerated is around the breasts. The totally androgynous style of the sixties has relaxed somewhat – perhaps men couldn't stand the maternal deprivation, when it came to it. But even with breasts, the emphasis is on the 'well-rounded' and 'firm' in keeping with the bulgeless body.

The most striking aspect of this body is that it is reminiscent of adolescence; the shape is a version of an immature body. This is not because with the increase in the earnings of young people, the fashion industry now has them in mind (though there may be an element of truth in this), because the ideal is not exactly a young girl. Rather it is an older woman who keeps an adolescent figure. Witness the eulogies over Jane Fonda's body; a woman of nearly fifty with the 'fantastic body' of a teenager.

This valuation of immaturity is confirmed by other practices concerned with rendering the female body sexually attractive. The practice of shaving under the arms and shaving the legs removes the very evidence that a girl has reached puberty. It is considered attractive that these 'unsightly' hairs are removed. Body hair is considered ugly and beauty advice strongly recommends shaving the body to restore pre-pubescent smoothness. A recent hair-removal advertisement spelled out the ideology: 'Go as Bare as You Dare. With Bikini Bare you can wear the briefest bikini, the shortest shorts or the new "thigh-high" cut swim suits with confidence.' Strange paradox here. Pubic hair appearing in its proper place is unsightly. Yet fashion is designed precisely to reveal this part.

The aim is constantly to produce smoothness, 'no razor stubble'. The aim of shaving legs is to produce these firm, lean, smooth objects which, naturally, have a far higher incidence on a rangy, sexually immature body than on an older woman.

It is no coincidence that this sexual ideal is an image which connotes powerlessness. Admittedly, the ideal is not of a demure, classically 'feminine' girl, but a vigorous and immature adolescent. Nevertheless, it is not a shape which suggests power or force. It has already been fairly widely documented how women often choose (albeit unconsciously) to remain 'fat' because of the power which somehow accrues to them.[1] And it is certainly true that big women can be extremely imposing. A large woman who is not apologizing for her size is certainly not a figure to invite the dominant meanings which our culture attaches to femininity. She is impressive in ways that our culture's notion of the feminine cannot tolerate. Women, in

[1] See S. Orbach, *Fat is a Feminist Issue* (Hamlyn, 1979).

other words, must always be seen as women and not as impressive Persons with definite presence.

The cultural ideal amounts to a taboo on the sexually mature woman. This taboo is closely related to other ideologies of sexually appropriate behaviour for men and women. Historically, for instance, the law has had difficulty in recognizing women as sexually responsible individuals. In the statutes of the law, in fact, it is only men who are deemed capable of committing sexual crimes, and this is not just because it is indeed men who tend to attack women. These legal ideologies are constructed on the belief that only men have an active sexuality, therefore only men can actively seek out and commit a sexual crime. Women in these discourses are defined as the sexually responsive or passive victims of men's advances. Actually (as much recent feminist writing on the law has made us realize) the *workings* of the law do embrace very definite beliefs about female sexuality.[2] In rape cases, there are frequent attempts to establish women's culpability, to establish that women 'asked for it' in some way, and gave out messages which invited a male sexual attack. Thus even though the *statutes* of the law appear to protect women against men's active sexuality, in fact the *workings* of the law often put women on trial and interrogate them about their degree of responsibility for the attack.

The ideology in the legal treatment of rape corresponds closely with general ideologies about masculine and feminine behaviour. It is acknowledged that women have a sexuality, but it is a sexuality which pervades their bodies almost as if *in spite of themselves*. It is up to women to protect themselves by only allowing this sexual message to be transmitted in contexts where it will be received responsibly, that is, in heterosexual, potentially permanent situations. This is why the defence of a rapist is often conducted in terms of attempting to cast doubt on a woman's sexual 'morality'. If she can be proved to have used her sexuality 'irresponsibly', then she can be suspected of having invited the active attack of the man. It is only women who have expressed their sexuality within the safety of the heterosexual couple who can be guaranteed the protection of the law.

The sexually immature body of the current ideal fits very closely into these ideologies. For it presents a body which is sexual – it 'exudes' sexuality in its vigorous and vibrant and firm good health – but it is not the body of a woman who has an adult and powerful

---

[2] See S. Edwards, *Female Sexuality and the Law* (Martin Robertson, 1982).

control over that sexuality. The image is of a highly sexualized female whose sexuality is still one of response *to* the active sexuality of a man. The ideology about adolescent sexuality is exactly the same; young girls are often seen as expressing a sexual need even if the girl herself does not know it. It is an image which feeds off the idea of a fresh, spontaneous, but essentially *responsive* sexuality.

But if this image is somewhat at variance with how the majority of women, especially the older ones, experience their sexual needs, their choices and their active wants, then how is it that this body image continues to prevail? How does that image continue to exist in women's lives, making them unhappy by upholding impossible ideals? How is it that these images have a hold when most women would also express extreme cynicism about advertising stereotypes and manipulation, not to mention knowledge of the techniques by which these body forms are sometimes achieved? (It is not just the real body that is subjected to the knife. Far more common is the cutting off of excess flesh on the photographic image.)

Perhaps the mechanism most important in maintaining women's concern with this ideal is that it is built on a *disgust* of fat and flesh. It is not just a simple case of an ideal to which some of us are close and others not, which we can take or leave. The ideal says as much about its opposite, because the war with fat and excess flesh is a war conducted in highly emotive language. And this language constructs the meanings and therefore the emotions which surround body image. The most basic point about this is that it is difficult to find a non-pejorative word to describe what after all is the average female shape in a rather sedentary culture. When it comes down to it, 'plump', 'well-rounded', 'full', and so on all sound like euphemisms for fat and therefore carry negative connotations. No one wants to be plump when they could be firm; it would be like choosing to be daft when you could be bright. But perhaps more important is that language pertaining to the female body has constructed a whole regime of representations which can only result in women having a punishing and self-hating relationship with their bodies. First, there is the fragmentation of the body – the body is talked about in terms of different parts, 'problem areas', which are referred to in the third person: 'flabby thighs . . . they'. If the ideal shape has been pared down to a lean outline, bits are bound to stick out or hang down and these become problem areas. The result is that it becomes possible, indeed likely, for women to think about their bodies in terms of parts, separate areas, as if these parts had some separate life of their

own. It means that women are presented with a fragmented sense of
the body. This fragmented sense of self is likely to be the foundation
for an entirely masochistic or punitive relationship with one's own
body. It becomes possible to think about one's body as if it were this
thing which followed one about and attached itself unevenly to the
ideal outline which lingers beneath. And the dislike of the body has
become pathological. The language used expresses absolute disgust
with the idea of fat. Fat is like a disease: 'if you *suffer* from cellulite
. . .' The cures for the disease are even worse. The body has to be
hurt, made to suffer for its excess. *Company* magazine reports on
'Pinching the Fat Away'. Pummelling is regularly recommended, as
is wringing out and squeezing: 'Use an oil or cream lubricant and
using both hands, wring and twist the flesh as though you were
squeezing out water, then use fists to iron skin upwards, kneading
deeper at the fleshier thigh area' (*A–Z of Your Body*). And under the
title of 'Working Hard at Looking Good' we are told about actress
Kate O'Mara's 'beauty philosophy': 'I'm determined to do all I can
to help myself. If I cheat on my regime, I write myself abusive notes.
Anyway, all this masochistic stuff gives me a purpose in life'
(*Cosmopolitan*).

It is almost as if women had to punish themselves for existing at
all, as if any manifestation of this too, too-solid flesh had to be
subjected to arcane tortures and expressions of self-loathing.

I have already suggested that one of the reasons behind this self-
disgust may be the conflict surrounding the cultural valuation of the
sexually immature image. It seems as though women have to punish
themselves for growing up, for becoming adults and flaunting their
adulthood visibly about their bodies. It is as if women feel that they
are too big, occupying too much space, have overgrown their
apportioned limits. And a punishment is devised which internalizes
the negative values which this society has for such women. It is of
course sensual indulgence which is seen as the root cause for women
overspilling their proper space. Women who feel themselves to be
overweight also invariably have the feeling that their fatness demon-
strates weakness and greed. Being fat is tantamount to walking
around with a sandwich board saying, 'I can't control my appetite.'

This belief is fostered by the slimming industry and by the
literature on fatness. Yudkin, for instance, in the *A–Z for Slimmers*,
writes: 'It's not very nice having to admit you are fat. It's much
more attractive to suppose that the extra weight isn't due to
overeating but is caused by fluid retention . . .' And *Slimmer*

magazine ran a spread asking whether children were helpful when their mothers were dieting. They gave a sample of the answers: 'An eight-year-old concerned about his mother's figure is Daniel Hanson of Ashford, Middlesex. "I'm not going to let my mum have any more sweets," he declared firmly. "I want her to be thin like other mums." And nine-year-old Kerry Wheeler says of her mother, "She's looking thinner now, but we can't stop her eating sweets. I have to take them away from her." '

At the heart of these caring offspring's anxieties about their mother's body shape, and at the heart of the discourses on the ideal body, lies a paradox. The *sexual* ideal of the slim, lithe, firm body is also a statement of self-denial, the absence of any other form of sensuality. This adds a further dimension to the cultural connotations of immaturity. The ideal body is also evidence of pure devotion to an aesthetic ideal of sexuality, a very limited aesthetic ideal. Ideal sexuality is limited sensuality; the ideal excludes any form of sensual pleasure which contradicts the aspiration for the perfect body. Again it is a statement about a form of sexuality over which women are assumed to have no control, since it is a statement about not having grown up and pursued other pleasures.

The ideal promoted by our culture is pretty scarce in nature; there aren't all that many mature women who can achieve this shape without extreme effort. Only the mass of advertising images, glamour photographs and so on makes us believe that just about all women have this figure. Yet the ideal is constructed artificially. There are only a very limited number of models who make it to the billboards, and the techniques of photography are all geared towards creating the illusion of this perfect body.

Somewhere along the line, most women know that the image is impossible, and corresponds to the wishes of our culture rather than being actually attainable. We remain trapped by the image, though, because our culture generates such a violent dislike of fat, fragmenting our bodies into separate areas, each of them in their own way too big. Paradoxically, though, this fragmentation also saves us from despair. Most women actually maintain an ambiguous relation to the ideal image; it is rarely rejected totally – it pervades fantasies of transforming the self. But at the same time, there's far more narcissistic self-affirmation among women than is sometimes assumed. Because of the fragmentation of the body into separate areas, most women value certain aspects of their bodies: eyes, hair, teeth, smile. This positive self-image has to be maintained against the grain for the dice are loaded against women liking themselves in this society. But such feelings do lurk there, waiting for their day, forming the basis of the escape route away from the destructive and limiting ideals which are placed on women's bodies.

The Mirror with a Memory

'The Mirror with a Memory'. This was the description given to the earliest practical photographic process perfected by Louis Daguerre in the 1840s. Daguerre's process made light act directly to produce an image by the use of lenses and light-sensitive plates. And, though contemporary photographic technique bears little resemblance to Daguerre's process, the belief remains that the photograph merely fixes and records for posterity the haphazard production of images by light, images which would otherwise remain the fleeting, subjective impression of an individual's vision.

With the production of people's likenesses through this process, the pen and ink outlines of history were fleshed out. 'Real people' made an appearance. The impermanence of the mirror image was replaced by the possibility that the mirror was looking back and that what it saw could be recorded. Photographic ideologies convince us that we can be both self and other. We can see ourselves and see how others see us.

Perhaps this is why women's relation to the photographic image is tense and loving, embodied in the fascination with the family snapshot and its record of people's likenesses. Women cherish snapshots. Not the boring ones, the views from the hotel bedroom and the sunsets over the sea; but the photos with people in them, other people and yourself, separately and together. And women destroy pictures of themselves, cut themselves off the edges. In every collection there's at least one picture where a disembodied hand rests lovingly on the shoulder of the photo's subject.

Guardians of the unwritten history of the family, women collect and keep photographs. Tied with ribbons, higgledy-piggledy in old chocolate boxes, or kept in orderly albums, photos are used as precious evidence of the existence of yourself and other people. Photo collections are used as evidence, the tangible proof of our genealogies. For those with humble origins, the birth of photography quite literally founds the family. Unbeknown to themselves, the women and men who moved in from the country and visited a photographic studio in Battersea, founded a veritable dynasty. History for most of us begins with these earliest photographs – the fearsome matriarch fading in her oval portrait, Grandfather enjoying his day-trip to Brighton, incomprehensible figures under palm trees (the proud souvenirs of humble clerks in the service of imperialism), a distant relative visiting in a car.

The keepers of these photos become the historians. They remember eccentricities to add to the paucity of the visual image, eccentricities beside which the Borgias pale. With the birth of photography, history becomes real, but above all the family becomes tangible. No longer a series of memories passed by word of mouth, the family becomes a gallery of characters to be understood and interpreted from their appearance. Where there might be a social history, there is instead a series of likenesses, a genealogical process leading inevitably to our uniqueness.

Taking and collecting photographs is a perpetual attempt to record and capture transient moments, to fix them and ensure their permanence. Beliefs about photography feed this impulse: 'Nothing is more precious than a happy memory and you can keep a delightful record of every unforgettable occasion using this superb Halina Camera' (Family Album Fashion Free Offer). The allegedly 'unforgettable' occasions seem to require a little aide- mémoire: so much so that you often hear complaints that family gatherings sometimes resemble amateur photography classes.

Photographs, of course, are never simply a record of the real likeness or innocent witnesses to events 'as they really are'. Photography is about as natural as a photograph of Granny in a 'kiss me quick' hat at Eastbourne when she never wore a hat and had only been to the seaside once in her life. But we are constantly persuaded that the photograph merely transcribes the real, that it is merely light rays captured by technology in place of the eye. But the moment seized by photography is a sight we never actually have. The speed of contemporary films means that the shutter fixes a still image when there is only movement in subjective vision. John Berger wrote, 'a photograph is a trace of appearances seized from the normal flow of the eye'.

Moreover, the form taken by the photograph is determined by distinct ideologies, and this is no less true for the casual snapshot than for the news photo: any photo involves choices about subjects, how they are organized and posed, such technical considerations as layout, framing, cropping, whether the photo is black and white or colour, and how much co-operation there is between photographer and subject. Family snapshots are submitted to two specific criteria. One is that certain moments are considered more significant than others, and the second is that, increasingly, the snapshot should be natural and unposed.

Jo Spence, the photographer, has greatly enhanced our

understanding of the symbolism behind choices for the family collection.[1] Certain moments and subjects are taken as significant, these being the moments of family solidarity. And women are photographed in roles and actions which affirm this solidarity – birth, fiancée, bride, mother. The portrayal of these symbolic stages is overdetermined by the stereotypical ways in which women are generally portrayed.

Looking at her own family album, Jo found herself posing, at the age of five, as Shirley Temple. All through her life, the snapshots echoed previous ways in which women had been represented. The kind of poses and the styles are influenced directly by religious, ideological and artistic conventions. Behind every new mother sits a Renaissance Madonna, and behind every young woman the contemporary 'glamorous' image. Doubtless there are few weddings in the 1980s that are not haunted by the spectre of the Royal Wedding. Women being much observed and defined cannot escape those coercive definitions even in their own homes.

And because snapshots are informed by general cultural definitions of women, they distort 'family' life. In snapshots there is no sign of labour, conflict, hardship, grief – no sign of sibling rivalry, anguished adolescence, or death. Where the snapshot is under the injunction to record happy moments of family solidarity, there is no attempt to deal with the deep underground streams of family emotions. There is somehow a tacit agreement that the world can be divided up into distinct experiences with distinct photographic conventions to illustrate them. So, we have happiness and solidarity in the family (snapshots) and we have 'social problems' which are not supposed to occur in the family and are recorded by 'professional' photographers for serious journals.

Family snapshots are not just governed by conventions about the subject. They are also increasingly under the injunction to be as natural as possible. There's a desire to produce a photo that's not posed, and shows people at their most relaxed. Photography has to be as unobtrusive as possible, so that a picture can be taken just as if it were a frozen look: 'The 110 Auto flip model is compact, lightweight, and ideal for slipping into a pocket or bag so you can take your family and friends by surprise' (Family Album Fashion Free Offer).

[1] See Jo Spence, 'Facing up to Myself' in *Spare Rib*, issue 68, March 1978. Jo Spence has also worked – in collaboration with Terry Dennett – on what it means to be a 'professional' photographer. See 'Remodelling Photohistory' in *Ten: 8*, Winter 1982.

Indeed, the drift towards the ever smaller camera is all part of the need to make technology invisible, to make the act of photography more and more like blinking. Modern photographic techniques have all been geared to produce a method which appears like an extension of the photographer. The camera will become an extension of the eye, secretly recording your own observation of 'spontaneous' events. Some developments even make the printing process appear like an extension of the brain; polaroid delivers its image as if it came from the back of the brain on a piece of light-sensitive paper.

Early photography, with its long exposure times, offered possibilities for participation by the subject in determining their own postures. But this has been obliterated as photography is increasingly valued for having 'caught people off their guard'. The language is revealing. Like most photographic metaphors, it suggests possession. We talk of 'capturing' happy events, 'seizing' fleeting moments, snapping funny moments and of photography as record, witness, evidence, almost as if a crime had been committed. Such language tells about the desire to perfect this personal 'grasp' of reality, a grasp which doesn't consult its subjects. It shouldn't surprise us that photography should try to obliterate its possessive nature by trying to be as unobtrusive as possible.

But why in all this are women so central, so crucially involved? Photography is permissible looking when the photograph is removed from the context where staring would be unacceptable. In our society men can and do stare – at women. It is a look which confers a mastery. It represents a right to assess, pass judgment and initiate or invite on the basis of that judgment. Women do not stare at people in this way, we are not the subjects of look but the objects. With photographs, however, we can look and look, not just at men but at everyone. We can feed off appearance, and reclaim the visible world.

In particular the belief that the photograph is the true view of the other, 'the mirror with a memory', appears to allow us an objective take on an otherwise subjective but crucial aspect of our world. The image for women, being the sex which is defined and made the subject of aesthetic judgment, is decisively enmeshed in the power-relations of looking. From the earliest age, women are alerted to the fact that the mirror might look back, that in our image may lie the decisions as to whether we will be loved. How could women avoid such a conclusion? All around, our culture parades woman's worth in terms of her correspondence with the prevailing ideal; all around language offers terms in which to think about women visually; and all around the media emphasize the importance of perfecting the appearance. And our sexuality too follows this pattern. Since it should not be active, seeking, decisive, it should be responsive; our sexuality should aim at eliciting the reaction.

But the mirror is unreliable. The first image we form of ourselves in the mirror is an object of pleasure. We delight in the possibility of that unified image. And the parents of the small child encourage that pleasure, celebrate the infant's first apprehension of its likeness in the mirror. Moreover, the likelihood is that the child resembles one or other of its parents, the adults most closely involved in caring for it. (This is the resemblance which is sought across family portraits.) So women can never wholly forget that first love, however much the image may differ from prevailing ideals. Yet everything around us engenders insecurity in the image, calls on us to work and improve, threatens us, if we do not improve, with the loss of love.

In this complex web, the photograph offers itself as the record of what the mirror sees, the chance to see ourselves and those around us as others see us. Even if the situations are improbable, the combinations of people unlikely, women treasure these images because they appear to be the objective record of how we are all seen and valued.

Women lovingly collect photographs of people because they appear to offer us a position in the world by which we feel judged; they appear to admit us to the criterion by which the visual impression we create is judged.

We are lured to photographs as witnesses of how we exist in the world, by the possibility of occupying the position of the other who judges and records. But photographs trick us. Instead of objective record, we encounter absence. Photography confronts us, most of all, with a sense of images of something which is no longer happening, is no longer there. It recalls the possibility of our own absence, and death, and fails to yield up a view of a full world and our existence in it.

And to cover this absence, we deny it and find a way round to restore our love for our images and the full world which accompanied our early narcissism. We abolish the images which don't correspond to our mirror faces and fall back in love with ourselves as if there were no cultural super-ego and no absences or separations. And we set about collecting likenesses of our antecedents and children which feed our narcissism and re-create an undamaged world. We view new-born babies and toddlers with all the narcissistic gratification which we first invested in our own likenesses. Surrounded by photographs we attempt to re-create an infantile world, a world where there is no critical super-ego and where we have not encountered the pain of separation and loss.

Pouts and
Scowls

COMPANY

THE LIVELIER MAGAZINE

May 1982 50p

THE BABY BARRIER
WHAT HAPPENS IF HE WANTS ONE MORE THAN YOU?

NEW JOB BLUES
HOW TO GET THROUGH THOSE FIRST TREACHEROUS DAYS

TREAT YOURSELF TO THE FRONTIER LOOK
OUR DENIM SKIRT AND JACKET SAY IT ALL FROM ONLY £12.50

CASHING IN ON THE RECESSION
TRY A LITTLE LATERAL THINKING

WHY DO WOMEN SMILE SO EASILY?

HOP ON THE WILLIAM HURT BANDWAGON
HE'S HOLLYWOOD'S HUNKY ANSWER TO THE ENGLISH ARISTO

AN OFFENSIVE GUIDE TO BAD TASTE

THE JOY OF THE ALBUM
SIX-PAGE RECORD COLLECTOR'S SPECIAL

A crucial change has overtaken the representation of the female face in advertising or women's magazines. The models have stopped smiling. Angela Carter noted the change as early as 1975. 'This season's is not an extrovert face. Because there is not much to smile about this season? Surely. It is a bland, hard, bright face' (*New Society*, 1975). But now even the fashion commentators and women's magazines themselves are deep in consideration of why this change has occurred:

Remember the days when every news-stand was alive with white teeth, flashing deep and crisp and even, on everything from high fashion glossy to mass circulation weekly? Now rows of unsmiling faces gaze out from these same covers, lips firmly closed over thousands of pounds' worth of orthodontic dentistry, expressions ranging from outright scowl to helpless dreamy, hunted or gently resigned.
                                        A. de Courcy, *Standard*, 31 August 1982

Women's magazine covers used to be dominated by beliefs from fashion photography about how to convey a glamorous image which would 'appeal to women's fantasies'. It was believed that the smile was crucially important. Inviting and seductive, the smile was supposed to make familiar the face in the wilderness, on the head without a body, on the person without a social setting. But this face has now been subtly transformed; the face in the wilderness is above all a glum face. If not exactly aggressive, the look is now consistently resistant.

It is a curious turnabout when you consider that one of the first feminist objections to advertisements was to the stereotypical portrayal of the smiling woman, submissive and anxious to please. Some commentators have suggested that this new glum look is indeed a response to this feminist critique: 'There is nothing ingratiating about the crop-haired little blond whose deadpan streetwise expression stares from the front of this month's *Company*. Editor Maggie Goodman . . . believes this is due partly to fashion, partly to feminism' (A. de Courcy, op. cit.).

But if the smile was a gesture of female submission, it is hard to see its opposite as a feminist resistance to such submission. Instead it arises from new and very definite ideologies as to what is attractive. And the criterion as to what is considered attractive arises primarily within the fashion and advertising industries themselves. There is every indication that magazines and newspapers actively invite more smiling models, but are repulsed by a dominant belief on the part of the models and the photographers as to what constitutes attractiveness. *Cosmopolitan*'s editor is reported as saying, 'I think it would be much better if they did smile. Our message is that times may be tough but there is something you can do about it – and a smile puts that across. However, *the models just won't* – I tear my hair about it' (A. de Courcy, op. cit. my emphasis). The editor of *Company* likewise confirms that the serious look is coming not from editorial policy but from the models and the photographers: 'It's easier to look tough than to smile. So models don't and *even if they wanted to, photographers wouldn't let them*' (ibid., my emphasis).

Where then have these definite criteria arisen, if not as a response to recession or to feminism? The most striking thing about the look that greets us whichever way we turn is that it is unresponsive and uncompromising. It may range from a faint flicker of amusement to almost outright aggression, but it is always resistant. It is a look which if it came your way in the course of a relationship would warn you that you were in for a rough evening.

This now fashionable look is remarkably similar to representations of female sexual expressions which have long dominated pornography, which is aimed at men. Even in the heyday of the smile in women's magazines, the look in pornography was invariably unsmiling. Occasionally there may be a trace of a smile or a dreamy look of sexual pleasure, but on the whole sex is signified as a serious business. Women are often presented as introverted, self-absorbed, busy in the act of touching or admiring self. But when, in pornography, a full look is directed towards the camera, it is a stare, unwavering, usually unsmiling, meeting the voyeuristic look of the camera unflinchingly.

Yet there's no way in which we could see this expression as 'streetwise' or proto-feminist; the way the look is directed, the posture of the body, are both weighed down with sexual meanings. It is quite clear that the photographs are posed, framed and lit according to certain conventions which communicate sexual alertness. The look is arranged according to certain codes: the eyes are narrowed to denote sexual interest; the mouth slightly opened to denote sexual arousal. Then the woman's body is arranged in ways to expose parts to the camera as if it was making love to her. The look of the porn model to the camera puts the viewer in the position of lover, confronting a stare that is simultaneously inviting and challenging.

It seems to me that the look now dominating women's magazines in general has come direct from pornography. For it is not just the look, but the postures in the advertising or display of fashions which directly parallel pornographic criteria of attractiveness. General fashion now frequently shows women in postures drawn directly from pornography. Shots emphasize bottoms, or reveal women lying in inviting postures, legs apart.

Given that there are intimate connections between the world of models, photographers and pornographers, it shouldn't really be surprising to find 'glamour photography' drawing on codes and conventions from pornography. Professional ideologies within photography tend to obscure this, though. Until recently photographers always seemed to be insisting that there was a marked difference between the kind of glamour photography aimed at women and that aimed at men.

The posture and expressions from pornography have nothing to do with feminism and everything to do with prevailing ideals of sexual attraction. The look, above all, is meant to denote the ultimate state of sexual arousal; the woman's seriousness denotes readiness for sex. If the expression appears to say, 'Fuck you,' it actually reads, 'Fuck me.' The expression shows a state of sexual readiness which is there with or without invitation. The look of defiance, the pouting and scowling faces, are part of the current tendency to represent women as attractive *whether or not they work at it.* Indeed, the look ultimately says, 'It's not because of my invitation that you will want me. You will want me anyway.' We are meant to read off from the narrowing of the eyes, the perfection of the skin, the posture of the body, that this is a person confident of sexual response whether or not it is sought.

If feminists criticized the stereotype of the simpering and ingratiating femininity which used to dominate woman-directed images, this new scowling face is no less problematic. Here again is a representation of female sexuality which reinforces ideas about female passivity. Like so many other areas of fashion, now even the face of woman is playing its part in telling us how men and women get together. On the basis of the exceptional looks of women, men will look, react, act. It matters not that these images are directed to women; the meanings of sexual readiness and arousal, spawned by pornography, have spread out to determine general standards of what is attractive.

I am reminded of the advertising campaign run by Gigi for their range of Loveable underwear. On one advertisement, the woman is shown dressed in glamorous but businesslike clothes. It's night-time and she's scowling into the camera, as if stopped for a moment as she goes about her business. In the right-hand corner, the same woman is shown in a posture directly taken from pornography. She's opening up her blouse to reveal her bra. Her hair is less severely styled. It falls softly around her face which is turned away from the camera, looking down, looking at her own body. The caption underneath reads, 'Underneath they're all loveable'. The suggestion is that however tough and resistant women appear they are still sexual, sensual, soft and loveable. In the larger picture the woman appears to be saying no to some sexual advance. But the message is clear. Beyond the look of resistance is sexual readiness; if she looks back fiercely, it's only because she's aroused. The message recirculated by such an advertisement is like the ideology that sometimes excuses rape: the woman is really ready for it.

It is hard to avoid the conclusion that the emergence of the sullen and scowling model has a lot to do with these beliefs. It is as if she's escaped from the normally tight boundary that exists between pornographic (illicit) sexual representations and those representations which are widely available for the perusal of both sexes. The female body is the place where this society writes its sexual messages. Nowhere is this more so than in pornography – a series of images which are used almost exclusively by men. Here men can, protected by the illusion that what they are seeing is illicit and out of the way of ordinary (mixed) society, write their fantasies and desires on women's ever-ready bodies. But fashion photography has taken over the meanings from that secret place, made them general. The challenging aroused face, ready to be overcome, is now all around us. The face says all too clearly that precious moves towards real autonomy for women have been contained. In the look of resistance lies a whole convention of submission.

Ideal Homes

There's a wide, light sitting-room with French doors opening on to a well-tended garden. The room has a pine ceiling with down-lighters; the walls are pale coloured and on them hang a few framed pictures. There are lots of big plants and two modern sofas. In the centre of the room is a glass table; in one corner, an ornate antique cabinet. This is the home of an architect, we are told, a home 'noted for the particular brand of elegance in furniture and decoration to be seen throughout'.[1]

The pictures are there to give us 'furnishing ideas'. If we can find out where to buy these furnishings (and can afford them), we too can acquire a 'stylish home'. 'Style' is something which some people have naturally, but thanks to such photographs all of us can find out what it is and where to get it.

Magazines like *Homes and Gardens* and *Ideal Home*, which deal in such images, are specialist magazines, like those aimed at men – *Custom Car* and *Hi-Fi* for instance. Home magazines, too, carry specialist advertising aimed at an interest group, those involved in the process of home-buying, home-improvement and decoration. But the general tenor of the articles makes it clear that women are taken to be the main consumers of such images. The Do-It-Yourself section of *Homes and Gardens* was at one time a detachable section, easily removed from the main bulk of the more feminine concerns: fashion and beauty, food, gardening and general articles like, 'Why do women always feel guilty?' And if specialist home magazines carry general articles for women, it is also the case that general women's magazines carry articles about homes and furnishing remarkably similar to those of the specialist magazines.

Here, then, is a regime of images and a particular form of writing aimed largely at women. And, as with fashion, home-writing encourages a narcissistic identification between women and their 'style'. The language of home-improvement in fact encourages an identification between women's bodies and their homes; houses like women are, after all, called stylish, elegant and beautiful. Sometimes the connections become more explicit, as when someone refers to 'Mr X and his decorative wife'. Adverts too play with these

[1] This and all subsequent quotations come from one of the following magazines: *Ideal Home*, December 1977, October 1980, December 1980, and May 1982; *Homes and Gardens*, July/August 1980, November 1980, March 1980; *Options*, July 1982, February 1983; *Good Housekeeping*, June 1982; *Company*, May 1982.

connections. One company advertised its new range of bath colours with the caption 'Our recipe calls for Wild Sage'; it showed a woman applying her make-up in a beautiful bathroom. Enforcing these connections makes one thing clear; the desire for the beautiful home is assumed to be women's desire.

The images and articles relating to home-improvements don't just show any old picture of any old house. There's a preferred kind of image and a very definite style of writing. Lifestyle is a term much favoured by home-improvement writers, and the activity of reading about and looking at other people's homes is essentially offered as a chance to peep into these lifestyles. Home-literature is essentially voyeuristic, a legitimate way of peeping through keyholes in a society where the private realm is kept so separate from public life. Through these images, women can look in on other people's decor, their furnishings, and pick up clues about how other people live. This is one of the few routes of access which women have into the private lives of people other than their immediate circle.

This keyhole voyeurism has two characteristic forms, forms which in fact turn up in all sorts of magazines, not just the specialist home magazines. One common mode is sneaking glimpses of the rich and famous, those alleged 'personalities' spawned by our society. In 'The Los Angeles home of Veronique and Gregory Peck' we get a quick peek at their 'elegant dining-room' which, 'strong, cool and dramatic', reflects 'something of the personalities behind it'. Indeed, more than all the writings about the love-lives of these personalities, ideal-home writing seems to unearth the most intimate form of revelations. After all, if you had seen the puce-coloured bedroom of Terry Wogan, would there be anything more to know?

The other kind of voyeurism, though, is rather more common. This is the scrutiny of the homes of the unknown, the ordinary people who have done up their homes in such exemplary ways. Unknown these people may be but unsuccessful they certainly aren't. Here we have hordes of successful individuals, 'a rising star amongst dress designers', or heterosexual professional couples, called Sue and Nick, or Jackie and Mike, who have worked miracles on their terraced London houses. These unknowns have actually achieved the ultimate accolade. Just by the sheer force of their 'personal style', their houses have been selected to teach the rest of us how.

The discourses of home-improvement have a very precise language without a precise referent. It is the photographic images which have to flesh out the meanings for the vague language of 'individuality', 'style', 'personality' and 'flair'. The articles talk of 'homes full of warmth and colour', 'elegant town houses', and describe how 'antique furniture combines happily with modern hand-crafted pieces, reflecting catholic tastes'. Home-improvements get praised when they achieve 'Today's look for Yesterday's houses'. Houses are 'lovingly restored to elegance and comfort' by their owners and admired for being 'a delightful combination of comfort and elegance, delicacy and crispness, that produces a relaxed formality'. The aims are 'colour and comfort', 'homely and handsome' but above all, 'stylish'.

Style, as with the fashion magazines, is always the name of the game. Style lies like a blanket across all the descriptions of houses and their decorations; 'Leonard Rossiter: we visit his stylish family town house'; 'Ceilings: Round off your room in style'; 'Strong on Style'; 'Stylish Alternatives'. We are told about a Victorian terraced house ready for demolition which 'a young couple' transformed into a 'tasteful and stylish home'. All the loving hard work, it seems, is worth it if they achieve the ultimate accolade, 'personal style'. Hard graft on 'daunting prospects' pays off if it adds up to a 'home of individual flair and style': 'It's been a lot of hard work but the final result is an original home with a very personal stamp on it. As she says, "It's so nice to come home to."'

Personal style – a strange paradox; individuals have it but we can all copy it. Personal style is, in reality, nothing other than the individual expression of general class taste and the particular ideals promoted by that class. No wonder the sign of an individual's uniqueness is so easily copied. The photographic images make it quite clear that there are consistent ideals even if the language remains stunningly vague. The kind of pictures taken, the kind of homes shown, offer very definite ideologies as to what domestic and private life is like. The reference to *ideal* homes is no light reference. Everything shown is at an ideal moment. The rooms shown are always curiously vacated: there's never a trace of mess, of dishes left unwashed, of beds unmade. Miraculously, the only signs of ubiquitous children are 'the children's bedroom, featuring a complex blue, black and white frieze by Osborne and Little' or 'a homework area for the children in a spare room, with light-stained fitted louvred cupboards'.

In spite of the offer of an intimate glimpse into a private home, all traces of life in that home tend in fact to be obliterated. The owners are evicted by the photographic regime. The house is photographed as it probably never is – tidy, sparkling clean, free of persons and their ephemera. These are not *homes* but *houses*. They are the finished products, the end of the long years of planning or 'loving restoration'. These are the houses that exist in the imagination during the years of painting, scrubbing, and hammering. The photographic regime captures the illusory moment of an 'after', that moment frequently imagined during all the hard work. The lure during such work is precisely this, a finished product. But even if such work were ever finished – and for most of us, it never is – a house that is truly lived-in could not sustain such perfection. To represent a lived-in home would destroy for ever more the illusion that a house could ever be finished and perfect. In a lived-in home, the satisfying moment of 'after' never occurs; 'after' is endlessly postponed until the fuzzy felt farm has been peeled off the carpet and the socks put into the dirty linen basket.

This regime of imagery represses any idea of *domestic* labour. Labour is there all right but it is the labour of decorating, designing and painting which leads to the house ending up in this perfect state. We hear about how much the wallpaper cost and how long it took to get the underlying wall into good condition. We don't hear about how long it took some woman to get the room tidy, or who washed the curtains. But then the photographs only show the ever-tidy, clean and completed home. The before and after imagery endorses the joint work of couples, the husband and wife team who plan, design and decorate the house. The suggestion is that together men and women labour on their houses. The labour is creative and the end product is an exquisite finished house-to-be-proud-of. Domestic labour, the relentless struggle against things and mess, completely disappears in these images. The hard and unrewarding ephemeral labour usually done by a woman, unpaid or badly paid, just disappears from sight. Frustration and exhaustion disappear. Instead a condition of stasis prevails, the end product of creative labour.

The only suggestion of the actual life of the inhabitants is in a vision of an empty dining-table. Inhabitants of ideal homes, it seems, do a lot of entertaining. Indeed, the empty dining-table surrounded by empty but waiting chairs is often presented as the hub of the house, an empty stage awaiting the performance. Could it be that 'entertaining' is the main way in which these inhabitants display their ideal homes? And could it be mere coincidence that cooking meals is also an activity which relies heavily on women's labour?

The centrality of the dinner party has been made more explicit by one magazine, *Options*. Here a 'lifestyle feature' caters for the less subtle voyeurs. In these features, we get to see the house and hear all about the home-improvements; we see the person (or couple) at work in their tastefully decorated studies; and then, *pièce de résistance*, we see pictures of their dinner parties *and* hear about their favourite menus. Such features virtually tell us the names of the guests; 'says Jeremy, "Since a lot of our friends are in the media or theatre, our house can look like a rest home for weary London celebrities."' And the articles leave us in little doubt about how enviable such lifestyles are meant to be; 'you can't spend long with the Pascalls without thinking they're the kind of sociable couple you wouldn't mind having on your Christmas card list'.

Not much thought is required to realize that we are being offered the styles and lifestyles of a very precise class fraction. It's not just that Nick and Jessica, Jeremy and Ann are middle-class. They are a very particular middle-class grouping. Indeed, my suspicions aroused, I found on closer examination that virtually everyone whose home appeared was involved in some way with the media. Publishing, advertising and television are high on the list for favoured subjects, but far and away the most likely target for an ideal-home spread were designers – graphic designers, fabric designers, architects. We see the home of Mary Fox-Linton, 'at the top of the tree as a decorator', and of 'Lorraine, a graphic designer of very definite tastes'. Then we learn about John: 'although he is a successful graphic designer running his own business, he and his wife . . . have made their home on a ten-acre farm high on the North Downs.' Even little professional subtleties are explained to the uninitiated: 'If you have ever wondered what the difference was between a designer and a decorator you can see it in Fanny's home, an artist's studio in Kensington.' And just as you begin to wonder why this group of people, you are told: 'It is, of course, easier to be original if you have the sort of design flair that makes Patrick Frey and his firm Patifet famous for its exquisite furnishing materials.'

Far be it from me to suggest that there may be a element of self-interest at work here. Perhaps it is just coincidence that these designers get such good publicity in the magazines? Perhaps information about these people just happens to find its way into the home-making magazines with only the smallest amount of help from

PR and communications companies? However it gets there we can
be sure of one thing. The groups presented are presumably remarkably like the people who produce the magazines. Self-referential
always, sycophantic sometimes, the journalism and images promote
a self-evident world where everyone knows what good taste and style
are. Here of course is the solution to the homogeneity of style. No
brightly coloured and large patterned wallpaper, no souvenirs, no
cheap mass-produced reproductions on the wall; the privileged
glimpses are all of one kind of person. In so far as working-class
homes do crop up, they are the subject of ridicule, material for an
easy joke: 'An index of proscribed examples of bad taste will be
regularly published. I promise that the following obvious candidates
will have fallen to the axe, hammer or incinerator – replica Victorian
telephones; onyx and gilt coffee tables . . . large red brandy glasses
with tiny porcelain kittens clinging to the side . . . Cocktail cabinets
. . . spare toilet roll covers . . . doorbells chiming tunes . . . Crazy
paving.' And as if to confirm my theories of a particular group
defining and setting the ideals, I discover that the writer of this
Company magazine article is none other than Jeremy Pascall, featured in the *Options* article quoted above, he of the dinner parties and
the media personalities.

This self-reflexive and self-congratulatory group has the hege-
mony over definitions of design, taste, style and elegance. The group
is not exactly the ruling class; they do not own the means of
production and they are by no means the most wealthy or financially
powerful people in the country. Yet they control the means of mental
production; they are the journalists, designers, graphic designers,
furnishers and publishers who can tell us what we should think,
what we should buy and what we should like. This grouping clearly
has enormous powers within society because the communications
media have enormous potential to decide our beliefs and tastes. But
it isn't even a matter of this group deciding our views. More
nebulous and perhaps more influential, these are the people who
design our homes, who show us how to decorate these homes, whose
material is on sale in the shops. These are the people whose tastes
dictate the very possibilities for much of our everyday lives.

And the standards set by this group are remarkably consistent.
The houses are all geared towards a conventional living unit. And
the decors are mere variations on a basic theme. The walls are plain;
there is minimal furniture; an absence of what is seen as clutter; and
light, open rooms. Indeed the ideal home is very much directed

towards a visual impact, and within this visual impact, towards a display of possessions. Furniture and decorations are chosen with an eye to how they match each other. Walls are painted with an eye to how to display an original painting or a framed print. Shelves and tables are arranged to show off expensive objects to their greatest advantage. Above all, the light colours and plain walls tend to demonstrate constantly how clean these walls are.

What is dismissed as bad taste in working-class homes is merely the arrangement of the home according to different criteria. In working-class homes, the pictures and colour are often on the walls, as wallpaper, not framed as possessions. Items are often displayed not to demonstrate wealth but because they have pleasurable associations. Here are souvenirs – memories of a good holiday; snapshots – memories of family and friends; and pieces of furniture chosen, not for overall scheme, but because they were liked in someone else's home. This is a different modality of furnishing, not necessarily concerned with the overall visual effect. Items of furniture are not always chosen to match but for different reasons. Here, you often find a his and hers corner – an ancient armchair which *he* refuses to get rid of, or a chiming clock which drives him mad but which *she* won't part with.

There's almost certainly an element of Oedipal drama in the obsessive ridiculing of working-class homes which goes on among the ideal-home exponents. Usually this media group are not from middle-class backgrounds but are the first 'educated' members of working-class or lower-middle-class backgrounds. Doubtless the determination to ridicule such homes arises from a determination to be different, to reject their background and all it represented. The class basis for this taste is always disguised in the writing, which insists there are such things as absolute good taste and good design. But class isn't the only thing disguised by the vagueness of labels of 'style' and 'elegance'.

The economic investment in home-restoration is also disguised by the language of loving restoration. The idea that home-improvement is merely the expression of individuality through good taste obscures the way in which this kind of restoration is a very real economic activity. People able to buy and restore houses, or build their own houses, are acquiring valuable possessions. These are the possessions which – as this group gets older, dies and leaves the houses to their children – will be creating a new elite – those who have no rent to pay as opposed to those who spend enormous proportions of their income on housing. For the house-owner, even their current property represents the creation of profit out of housing. Doing up one house, moving on to a bigger and more valuable one, with tax incentives on mortgages – home-restoration is certainly also gaining economic advantages over those who can afford only rented accommodation.

But perhaps the most impressive concealment effected by this particular style is women's relation to domestic work. We've already seen how the photography obscures domestic labour. But it is also the case that the style itself sets a goal which is the obliteration of any trace of labour or the need for labour. The style emphasizes the *display* of the home, its visual impact, which will reveal things about the personality which owns it. Any house requires intensive domestic labour to keep it clean, but plain walls, open fires and polished floors probably require more than most. To keep it spotless would either involve endless, relentless unrewarding labour or using another woman's low-paid labour. Because the ideal is so much that of *absence* of clutter and mess, of emphasis on visual impact, any sign of mess is a sign of failure.

The work which women usually put in on the home is obscured in other ways. Unlike the working-class home which sometimes visibly manifests the difference between the male and female personalities in the house, the ideal-home taste obliterates differences between men and women. The house is expected to be a uniform style. If there are two people living together, the house has to express the joint personality of the couple. And not only does the style obliterate evidence of two personalities but the articles are positively congratulatory that traditional divisions between the sexes have now gone. 'Peter and Alison Wadley,' we are told, 'have units made to their specification. "In design terms," Peter believes, "the kitchen represents an interesting problem because its status has changed over the last few years. It's no longer purely a working room – in most houses, all the family tend to gravitate there so it has virtually become a living-room."' Women, we are informed, are no longer consigned to the kitchen which becomes instead a living-room where everyone mucks in. Men, on the other hand, are just dying to get in there to try out their creativity. In short, the styles and articles about them are all about the abolition of conflict. The home is not a place where women are subordinated but a shared space, with domestic chores split happily between the sexes.

I don't wish to decry such a vision; it's just that I don't believe it.

Nothing in fact could be more mystifying about the real relations of the home, the minute and the major ways in which women continue to take responsibility for domestic life. Our society is rigidly divided on sex lines and this extends even into the home. While women's employment prospects are limited by male prejudice and by taking primary responsibility for child care, the home cannot be this fine place for all. However uncritical women may be of bearing the responsibility for the home, it is a rare woman who has *never* experienced home as a sort of prison. Confined there through limited possibilities, and bearing the awesome responsibility for the survival of young children, or torn by commitments to work and children, the home is often a site of contradiction between the sexes, not a display cabinet. Even in the most liberated households, women are well aware of who remembers that the lavatory paper is running out and who always keeps an eye on what the children are up to.

Because the home has been made so important for women, the decoration of the home matters a lot to women, perhaps more than it does to men. In a world of limited opportunies, there can be no doubt that in the construction of the house there are creative possibilities offered in few other places. It is also crucially important to women that they feel all right about where they live. But the creative aspects in women's wish to determine their environment have been submitted to a visual ideal whose main statement is the absence of the work they do, and absence of conflict about that work.

The Look

'I adore women and my eyes are in love with them,' J. H. Lartigue, photographer.

Mirror image/photographic image – pivotal points in the organization of female desire. Women's experience of sexuality rarely strays far from ideologies and feelings about self-image. There's a preoccupation with the visual image – of self and others – and a concomitant anxiety about how these images measure up to a socially prescribed ideal.

The preoccupation with visual images might appear to be the effect of a culture which generally gives priority to visual impact rather than other sensual impressions. The dominance of the visual regime has been augmented by the media surrounding us. Film, photography and television all offer forms of entertainment and communication based on the circulation of visual images, on the sale of the images and the meanings conveyed by them. With the development of techniques of mechanical reproduction and the technology of visual recording, Western culture has become obsessed with looking and recording images of what is seen.

This preoccupation with visual images strikes at women in a very particular way. For looking is not a neutral activity. Human beings don't all look at things in the same way, innocently as it were. In this culture, the look is largely controlled by men. Privileged in general in this society, men also control the visual media. The film and television industries are dominated by men, as is the advertising industry. The photographic profession is no less a bastion of the values of male professionalism. While I don't wish to suggest there's an intrinsically male way of making images, there can be little doubt that entertainment as we know it is crucially predicated on a masculine investigation of women, and a circulation of women's images for men.

The camera in contemporary media has been put to use as an extension of the male gaze at women on the streets. Here, men can and do stare at women; men assess, judge and make advances on the basis of these visual impressions. The ability to scrutinize is premised on power. Indeed the look confers power; women's inability to return such a critical and aggressive look is a sign of subordination, of being the recipients of another's assessment. Women, in the flesh, often feel embarrassed, irritated or downright angered by men's persistent gaze. But not wanting to risk male attention turning to male aggression, women avert their eyes and hurry on their way. Those women on the billboards, though; they look back. Those fantasy women stare off the walls with a look of urgent availability.

Some people – those concerned with maintaining the status quo – say that men's scrutiny of women is just part of the natural order. Man the hunter, a sort of cross between a rutting stag and David Bailey, roams the street, pouncing on whatever appeals to his aesthetic sensibility. Women, meanwhile, cultivate their looks, make themselves all the more appealing and siren-like, and lure men to a terrible fate – monogamy and the marital home. Such a theory appears to be a distortion – in reality, men often seem far more dependent on monogamous romantic sexual commitment than do women. But the theory also wilfully obscures the way in which sexual behaviour is formed according to social conventions and structures.

In this society, looking has become a crucial aspect of sexual relations, not because of any natural impulse, but because it is one of the ways in which domination and subordination are expressed. The relations involved in looking enmesh with coercive beliefs about the appropriate sexual behaviour for men and women. The saturation of society with images of women has nothing to do with men's natural appreciation of objective beauty, their aesthetic appreciation, and everything to do with an obsessive recording and use of women's images in ways which make men comfortable. Clearly this comfort is connected with feeling secure or powerful. And women are bound to this power precisely because visual impressions have been elevated to the position of holding the key to our psychic well-being, our social success, and indeed to whether or not we will be loved.

Men defend their scrutiny of women in terms of the aesthetic appeal of women. But this so-called aesthetic appreciation of women is nothing less than a decided preference for a 'distanced' view of the female body. The aesthetic appeal of women disguises a preference for *looking* at women's bodies, for keeping women separate, at a distance, and the ability to do this. Perhaps this sex-at-a-distance is the only complete secure relation which men can have with women. Perhaps other forms of contact are too unsettling.

Thus the profusion of images of women which characterizes contemporary society could be seen as an obsessive distancing of women, a form of voyeurism.[1] Voyeurism is a way of taking sexual pleasure by looking at rather than being close to a particular object of desire, like a Peeping Tom. And Peeping Toms can always stay in control. Whatever may be going on, the Peeping Tom can always determine his own meanings for what he sees. Distanced he may be, but secure he remains. Is this why one of the startling 'discoveries' made by twentieth-century sexology was the widespread use of sexual imagery, even during sexual intercourse itself? Turning back the sheets on the twentieth-century bed, sexology found a spectacle of incompetent fumbling and rampant discontent with 'doing it'. Heterosexuality it seemed was hovering on the edge of extinction, saved only by porn in the sock drawer, or by the widespread availability of images which could be substituted in fantasy for the real things. Perhaps in the images, the meanings are fixed and reassuring; perhaps only in the images could true controlling security be reached?

Attraction to images of women's bodies presented as ideal types is none other than an attraction to a sight which is in some way reassuringly pleasurable. And we've seen that the prevailing visual ideal is invariably an aesthetic ideal which conveys the prevailing values about sexual behaviour. Today's ideal is immaturity, a modern variant of feminine passivity. Because the female body is the main object of attention, it is on women's bodies, on women's looks, that prevailing sexual definitions are placed. The 'aesthetic sex' is the subordinate sex because beauty like truth is one of those empty terms, filled by the values of a particular society at a given historical moment. So when a woman is upheld by society as beautiful, we can be sure she expresses, with her body, the values currently surrounding women's sexual behaviour. The emphasis on women's looks becomes a crucial way in which society exercises control over women's sexuality.

Strict control over women's sexuality seems to be a characteristic of male-dominated societies. Marriage, for instance, often operates to secure women's labour and reproductive capacity to the advantage of men. In some societies the control of women is very direct – restrictions on movement, like foot-binding, rituals of exclusion, like purdah, the imposition of terrible punishments for adultery. In our society, the coercion is much more hidden and probably all the more

---

[1] For a summary of ideas about cinema as a voyeuristic activity, see J. Ellis, *Visible Fictions*, Routledge and Kegan Paul, 1982.

insidious. The last hundred years have seen less and less direct
control on women's morality and fertility. Indeed, Western society
prides itself on its 'advanced' morality. Some of the West's boasts of
'freedom' are based precisely on a boast of sexual freedom, a
freedom from archaic traditional morality. Sexual freedom is supposed to mean that individuals are free to follow their preference for
sexual partners without reference to the wishes of the community,
the family or the state. Individuals are supposed to be drawn to one
another without having to take into account property considerations
or political considerations.

Here in the West, then, we have a spontaneous and true sexual
morality. Untrammelled by ancient conventions, Cupid's dart is free
to enter where it will. But the coercion exercised on women by the
cultural obsession with women's appearances is precisely what is
disguised by such beliefs. When we hear talk of freedom to choose
sexual partners, we can be sure we'll also hear talk of visual appeal,
the mysterious alchemy which strikes from the blue at the most
awkward moments. And here's the coercion. Because women are
compelled to make themselves attractive in certain ways, and those
ways involve submitting to the culture's beliefs about appropriate
sexual behaviour, women's appearances are laden down with cultural values, and women have to form their identities within these
values, or, with difficulty, against them.

There's no simple matter of men imposing these meanings on
women who can then take them or leave them depending on
what they had for breakfast. Women are, more often than not,
preoccupied with images, their own and other people's. However
unconsciously, most members of this society get the message that
there's a lot at stake in visual impact. Most women know to their
cost that appearance is perhaps the crucial way by which men form
opinions of women. For that reason, feelings about self-image get
mixed up with feelings about security and comfort. Self-image in
this society is enmeshed with judgments about desirability. And
because desirability has been elevated to being the crucial reason
for sexual relations, it sometimes appears to women that the whole
possibility of being loved and comforted hangs on how their
appearance will be received.

Surely, it is this meshing with visual appearance of questions of
desirability and promises about security and comfort that accounts
for women's deep fascination with the visual images? This would
surely account for what has previously been recorded as women's

narcissism. Narcissism is certainly a useful notion, but it is crucially limited as an explanation of women's relation to images. Narcissus, it will be remembered, was a mythological character who was captivated by, indeed fell in love with, his own self-image, his reflection in a pool. It has been suggested that all children pass through a narcissistic phase where they become entranced by their own self-image.[2] The phase is supposedly characterized by the infant's fascination with its mirror image. This mirror phase in fact offers the child the first possibility of a unified sense of self, a unified identity, whereas prior to this stage the child had been dominated by motor unco-ordination and was awash with contradictory impulses over which it had little control. This glorious self-love provides the child with the first possibilities of an identity, with a self which could act on its surroundings and manipulate things to its advantage. In so-called normal development, another libido arises, existing beside this self-love. The other libido is that directed outwards towards another person or object.

Freud casually added to his account of the development of all humans that women were, however, 'more narcissistic'; 'nor does (their) need lie in the direction of loving, but of being loved; and the man who fulfils this condition is the one who finds favour with them'.[3] This assertion of women's greater narcissism has been left largely unchallenged, because at one level it appears so accurate. Indeed, the term has even been adopted to explain the process which is supposed to occur when women are bombarded with images of other women – in films, on TV, in the bulk of advertisements. As with the use of women's faces as icons on women's magazines, it is often assumed that women *identify* with these images rather than *desire* them, as men might confronted with similiar images. A narcissistic identification is supposed to take place; women like looking at glamorous and highly sexualized images of other women because these images are meant to function like a mirror. The image like a mirror reflects back to women their own fascination with their own image.

True though it is that women, especially young women, are deeply concerned with their own images, it is radically incorrect to liken women's relation with media images to the happy state of Narcissus. Women's relation to their own self-image is much more likely to be dominated by discontent. We have only to turn to the

[2] See S. Freud, *On Narcissism*, in Standard Edition, Vol XIV.
[3] S. Freud, op. cit., p. 89.

problem pages of *Jackie*, the magazine for teenage girls, to hear a howl of dissatisfaction – 'I'm not attractive enough.' And Jane Fonda (in her *Work Out Book*) summarizes the disappointment, leading so quickly to obsession, which characterizes adolescence:

From as early as I can remember my mother, her friends, my grand-mother, my governess, my sister – all the women who surrounded me – talked anxiously of the pros and cons of their physiques. Hefty thighs, small breasts, a biggish bottom – there was always some perceived imperfection to focus on. None of them seemed happy the way they were which bewildered me because the way they were seemed fine to my young eyes.

In pursuit of 'the feminine ideal' – exemplified by voluptuous film stars and skinny fashion models – women it seemed were even prepared to do violence to themselves. My mother, for example, who was a rather slender, beautiful woman, was terrified of getting fat. She once said if she ever gained weight she'd have the excess flesh cut off!

Fascination there may be, but there's certainly no straightforward indentification which women experience with the multitude of images of glamour women. Instead, advertisements, health and beauty advice, fashion tips are effective precisely because some-where, perhaps even subconsciously, an anxiety, rather than a pleasurable identification, is awakened. We take an interest, yes. But these images do not give back a glow of self-love as the image in the pool did for Narcissus. The faces that look back imply a criticism.

Women's relation to these cultural ideals, and therefore to their own images, is more accurately described as a relation of narcissistic damage. Even women's relation to their own mirror image is retrospectively damaged by that critical glance of the cultural ideal. Over the mirror always hangs the image of the socially approved, massively consumed, widely circulated image of the generic Woman. She alone it seems is guaranteed an easy ride through life, guaranteed the approval of all and safe in expecting uncritical love. Only she is guaranteed to recapture that happy childhood state, where child and adults alike gloried in the child's image.

Advertising in this society builds precisely on the creation of an anxiety to the effect that, unless we measure up, we will not be loved. We are set to work on an ever-increasing number of areas of the body, labouring to perfect and eroticize an ever-increasing number of erotogenic zones. Every minute region of the body is now exposed to this scrutiny by the ideal. Mouth, hair, eyes, eyelashes, nails, fingers, hands, skin, teeth, lips, cheeks, shoulders, arms, legs, feet –

all these and many more have become areas requiring work. Each area requires potions, moisturizers, conditioners, night creams, creams to cover up blemishes. Moisturize, display, clean off, rejuvenate – we could well be at it all day, preparing the face to meet the faces that we meet.

This is not only the strict grip of the cultural ideal; it is also the multiplication of areas of the body accessible to marketing. Here, areas not previously seen as sexual have been sexualized. And being sexualized, they come under the scrutiny of the ideal. New areas constructed as sensitive and sexual, capable of stimulation and excitation, capable of attracting attention, are new areas requiring *work* and *products*. Advertisements set in motion work and the desire for products; narcissistic damage is required to hold us in this axis of work and consumption.

Any visit to a hairdresser's tends to deliver up a little drama, an exemplary spectacle about the relation between the cultural ideal and the work women do on themselves. The mini-drama is always conducted around the mirror. First the client is sat in front of the mirror – 'How would you like it?' Then the mirror disappears – 'Come this way and have your hair washed.' Bedraggled but hopeful, the client returns to the mirror – the work is about to begin. And the final product? Well, how many times have you seen, or been, the client who to the amazement of the assembled company berates the hairdresser for the disaster visited on her head? Is it that in disappearing from the mirror the client imagines the *ideal* transformation, the work that will bring her mirror image into line with what she imagines it could be? Is the anger and disappointment just rage at the distance between self-image and that critical ideal that hangs menacingly beside us?

There is then, for women, an ambivalence between fascination and damage in looking at themselves and images of other women. The adult woman neer totally abandons the love which the little girl had for her own image, in the period of narcissistic glory. But this culture damages the glory, turns it into a guilty secret. The girl-child discovers herself to be scrutinized, discovers herself to be the defined sex, the sex on which society seeks to write its sexual and moral ideals. She learns that in this scrutiny might lie the answer to whether she will be loved.

Where women's behaviour was previously controlled directly by state, family or church, control of women is now also effected through the scrutiny of women by visual ideals. Photography, film and television offer themselves as transparent recordings of reality. But it is in these media where the definitions are tightest, where the female body is most carefully scripted with the prevailing ideals. Women internalize the damage created by these media; it is the damage of being the differentiated and therefore the defined sex. Women become *the sex*, the sex differentiated from the norm which is masculine. Women are the sex which is constantly questioned, explained, defined. And as the defined sex, women are put to work by the images. The command created by an image-obsessed culture is 'Do some work! Transform Yourself! Look Better! Be more erotic!' And through this command to meet the ideal, our society writes one message loud and clear across the female body. *Do not act. Do not desire. Wait for men's attention.*

PART II

THE MOUTH

Sweetheart

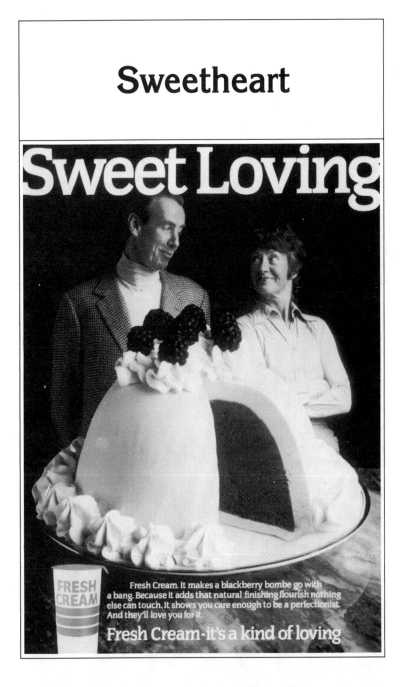

Sweet Loving

Fresh Cream. It makes a blackberry bombe go with a bang. Because it adds that natural finishing flourish nothing else can touch. It shows you care enough to be a perfectionist. And they'll love you for it.

Fresh Cream-it's a kind of loving

FRESH CREAM

Something about loving reminds us of food. Not any old food, not potatoes or lemons, but mainly sweet things – ripe fruits, cakes, and puddings.

Terms of endearment frequently refer to food: honey, sweetheart, peach, sugarplum. Even 'darling' appears to be a word which was also once used to describe a type of apple. And frequently there are deliberately absurd endearments, again making direct reference to food. Like the French *petit chou* (little cabbage), English makes affectionate reference to ducks, sausages and gooseberries. Sweet food, especially, has close links with romance; chocolates are a standard gift between lovers. But American society turned the love affair into a veritable trip to the confectionery shop: sweetie, sweetiepie, sugar, honeybunch, lollipop – the staple diet of familiarity.

Do we detect a note of cannibalism here? Certainly. Something about the sensations of sexual familiarity seem to evoke memories of food. Not only are the objects of affection like food, 'apple of the eye' or 'cream in my coffee', but the language suggests that the desire for sexual relations is like the desire for food. We have sexual *appetites*, we *hunger* for love, we *eat* out our hearts, *feast* our eyes and have *devouring* passions. And like any meal, we can overdo it and expect a bout of lovesickness.

Sexuality probably carries these alimentary overtones because the infant's earliest sensual experiences are closely connected with being fed and cared for, the activities also ensuring survival. Since Freud, we have become familiar with the idea of infantile sexuality, with the idea that the process of caring for a small child is also a process involving that child's sexuality. With such a theory, it would not be surprising to find sexual intimacy awakening memories of the first experiences of sexuality, where sensual and sexual gratification was associated with feeding.

There's more at work here than a straightforward metaphor – sexual familiarity is like the infantile satisfactions. Because as well as being a particular kind of language, food endearments are reserved for particular kinds of relationships and used by people in particular situations. And, on the whole, the food which comes to mind is sugar-based.

Food endearments are usually reserved for what I would call a masculine/maternal use of language. By this I mean that the use of

Female Desire

food endearments as diminutives tends to characterize the speech of male lovers to their partners, or mothers to their family. Of course, it is always difficult to make such generalizations and especially so for this kind of intimate or private language. After all, one of the common by-products of intimacy between two people is that they often start mimicking each other's speech. So, with endearments, there are often couples who use exactly the same terms to each other, like nicknames blurted out occasionally in public, much to the embarrassment of the users.

Doubtless such people would say I'm wrong to attribute these forms of speech to particular groups. But infantile food endearments are used in the *habitual* speech of certain groups in certain positions and only in the acquired speech of other groups. One place where it is customary to hear such language is in the speech of mother to child; the other is the speech of men to their lovers. When women use these terms to each other, or to men, they assume the position implied by the discourse. Either they adopt a position of masculine power like Mae West, whose speech firmly places men in 'feminine' positions, or, if women use these terms to men, they relate to these men often as mothers to children.

Surely it is reasonable to emphasize the masculine origins of this gastronomic sexuality? For it is men who regularly make the connection between food and sexual partners. All the derogatory terms used by men about women make this connection. Women are referred to as 'dishes' or 'tarts', or compared to nurturing animals like 'cows' or 'sows'. If mothers use gastronomic endearments, there are probably two reasons. One is that the mother/child relationship, as it is lived out in this society, seems closely to mimic the sexual relations between men and women. Indeed, women often describe their feeling about children in terms directly reminiscent of desire and affection in sexual relations. Hearing women talk of a physical pleasure and love for their children as more adequate than a sexual relation is not infrequent either. But, *in addition*, there are many aspects of the mother/child relation which correspond directly to elements of the adult (hetero)sexual relationship. This is because there's a meshing of nourishment and sensual gratification between mother and child. The child takes food and comfort from the mother, but the mother also feeds off the child's need for her and the sensual pleasure. Infantile food endearments certainly reflect this close connection between nurturing, feeding and sexuality.

But for men, this connection is particularly strong, and it is a connection reinforced by the hierarchical division of labour in this society. The boy child in fact never loses the possibility of restoring the mother's body as sexual object, and therefore the possibility of regarding sexual gratification as a relationship of nurturing. In adult relationships, this possibility is often actually enforced. In the division of labour, women are coerced into being those who provide and nourish. Women prepare the food, cook it and serve it – all seen by a sexist society as an inevitable aspect of 'femininity'. The so-called adult sexual relationship in heterosexuality is played out in such a way that women continue to nurture and provide for men even as adults. Adult heterosexuality has more than a small resemblance to the tyranny of the child over its mother. It is no accident that adult men start referring to their wives as 'mother'.

Heterosexual gratification for men clearly evokes oral pleasures and this is reinforced by the fact that men's social power has appropriated women's labour to care and provide for them. 'The way to a man's heart is through his stomach' is one of those sayings which unknowingly reveals the connections which a given society makes between different things. And, for men, there's not such a rigid division between food and sex as there appears to be for women.

Food metaphors used by men are not all gentle, sensual diminutives. There's also a measure of sadism lurking beneath the surface. There's a language of devouring, gobbling up, feasting with the eyes, a language which suggests the desire not only to eat but perhaps to destroy the loved object. Melanie Klein, a psychoanalyst, uncovered an infantile fantasy of devouring the mother, of introjecting all of her body, a desire which in its turn awakens the fear that the mother will seek retribution and destroy the child.[1]

Could this be the reason why one of the oldest sexist jokes/ fantasies is of men being slowly poisoned by their wives? Women's equivalent fear in sexual relationships, on the other hand, is a fear of being eaten, of being destroyed and made invisible by the desire their sexual partner has for them. In exactly the same way as men associate women with food, the female fantasy has close correspondence with external social circumstances. Women *are* often rendered invisible by men, confined to the home, silenced by male dominance or just not heard when they speak in public. In short, women's domestic role does put them in danger of being devoured or

[1] See M. Klein, *The Psycho-analysis of Children*, The International Library of Psychoanalysis, 1932.

destroyed, of disappearing altogether. In giving out comfort and support within conventional structures, women do run the risk of becoming invisible in society.

But what are we to make of the particular kind of food by which women are described as objects of desire – the sugars, sweets and confectionery? This sweet-toothed Western sexuality clearly demands some explanation. Interestingly, this society doesn't have endearments like milky, cheesy or buttery. This is strange, given the fact that dairy products are central in Western diets (being virtually taboo in some Eastern societies, like China). Indeed, the connection between women and milk is used by men as an insult, the insult of 'cows' and 'sows'. Perhaps there has been a repression here, an attempt to avoid making explicit the incestuous reference behind food endearments.

As well as the avoidance of certain connections, sugar-based foods have a particular meaning in this society. They were not always part of Western diets. Cocoa (and therefore chocolate) and sugar-cane were among the exotic goods imported into the West as colonialist expansion intensified. To begin with, sugar was a luxury item, only available to the wealthiest groups. Like jewels and precious stones, sugar represented the valuable possessions of a society which initially traded with sugar-producing countries and then colonized them. Endearments making reference to such food carried the associations of great economic value, high price and luxury. Significantly, other loving endearments draw on exactly these connotations: female lovers are called precious, treasure, jewel and pearl.

The economic reference like the food reference has a definite historical and social reality, since sexual relations in this society have an economic basis. There's nothing necessarily making us dispense with our sexuality in monogamous couples. We do this because of social conventions and their emotional consequences. No, the economic value connoted by these terms of endearment stems from the fact that in this patriarchal society sexual relationships with women imply certain economic consequences. Women's labour has either been subjected to men's control – she works for his household, as in the feudal economy – or women's reproductive capacity is harnessed to a male-dominated household – her offspring take his name and come to represent his security. Yet women's labour is at the same time represented as inessential, of less significance than men's. This has been even more true over the last two centuries where women's labour has been devalued to an extraordinary degree. Men's labour is seen as value-producing, integral to the life of society; women's as peripheral to productive relations, significant only for reproduction.

Here again, food endearments have made certain links which reflect the ideologies at work in a male-dominated society. For sugar-based foods have never been integrated into our diet. Sweet foods are almost invariably served as separate courses, like puddings or cakes, not integrated into the main course. And sweets and confectionery are bought and consumed separately from essential nourishment. Sugar-based foods are consumed by an affluent and exploitative society as symbols of inessential luxury, as evidence of wealth and power.

Nourishment, possession, inessential luxuries. With a startling precision, our language makes links between the attitudes which place women under the domination of men in this society.

Kissing

There's a common assertion that kissing is the ultimate symbol of sexual passion. Kissing expresses a bond, the consummation of sexual attraction and desire. It is the most tender and erotic moment of any relationship. There are two less common assertions about kissing. One is that women are much more likely to be ambivalent about the pleasure of kissing than men. The second is that women kiss with their eyes shut far more frequently than men.

To kiss someone is to transgress the conventional distance which is kept between self and others in this society. Sexual kissing establishes a mode of relating which is based on touch and smell, which is physically intimate in ways quite beyond the little gestures of affection between friends and family. In most non-sexual relationships, it is customary for each person to have a personal space, a private zone which is invisible but carefully preserved by other members of the same society. In this society, the personal space is between eighteen and twenty-four inches. Any greater degree of intimacy can be quite distressing as in a crowded train or bus where we are pressed against strangers, having to touch and smell unknown bodies. People from other societies are sometimes perceived as rude and aggressive when they unknowingly transgress the unwritten laws of intimacy.

The conventional distance between self and others in this society is a distance which gives priority to a certain kind of visual impact. At this distance, 'imperfections', as this society insists on calling them – wrinkles, skin pores or irritated skin – can be concealed. This distance doesn't 'distort' the face; the nose doesn't look too big nor does one eye disappear nor are we treated to a view up a nostril. Conventional photography and cinema have mimicked this respectful distance, not getting so close that the face is distorted. And when there is a close-up, the intimate vision of the face is obliterated by make-up, seeking to maintain the visual impression formed at a distance where blemishes can't be seen.

Routine social intercourse denies immediate access to what other people feel and smell like. Impressions are formed mainly on the basis of appearance, although some fashion practices do try to flag a sense of someone's personal zone. Scent, for example, aims at awakening the sensual pleasure of smelling. As such, scent can be an overt advertisement for the wearer's personal zone. But even this invitation is double-edged. The smell of scent obliterates the actual

Female Desire

smells of the human body, disavows physical intimacy while appearing to invite it.

Sexual relations alone regularly transgress the barrier around each individual. A sexual relationship is by definition a relationship which includes the modalities of touch and smell, as well as other reasons for relating. And the kiss seals a crossing into this personal zone, a crossing into the empire of the senses. With the kiss, degrees of intimacy change. The feel and scent of a body, warmth and close contact, the possibilities of physical pleasure, all come into play. The sexual relationship in this society is the only permitted adult relationship which is conducted according to these criteria, engaging these pleasures.

These pleasures evoke the experiences of childhood. The child in its early state of dependency experiences the world primarily through physical contact. Bodily warmth, sensual gratifications, familiar smells; these are the important sensations of the child's early life. As the child grows, though, these pleasures are largely withdrawn. A child learns slowly that such sensations are banished until an 'adult' sexual relationship is formed, learns that most social relationships must be conducted without reference to these physical pleasures

Sexual kissing initiates the possibility that normal barriers can be broken. Kissing is exciting and erotic for precisely these reasons. It has the delicious taste of the entry into the forbidden, a feeling which signals the activation of hidden physical sensations and needs. But just as kissing is the exciting and erotic moment where a physical intimacy is activated, so it can also become a very problematic activity. Women often talk of how kissing is the first activity to be abandoned when a relationship gets on the rocks. Genital stimulation, it seems, is often much less problematic, a much less intimate form of penetration than penetration of the mouth. It is strange to imagine that the penis is somehow less personal than the tongue, but that's the way it seems to be. Comments from prostitutes give overwhelming confirmation of this; much pride is taken in never having kissed a client. No matter what other kind of bizarre sexual practice a man might require, it seems as if a kiss is a far greater loss of personal integrity.

Kissing is a voracious activity, an act of mutual penetration. Kissing offers women the chance actively to penetrate. But this act of penetration is sometimes described as provoking anxiety. Sometimes women are disturbed by their own 'aggressive' desire to penetrate. More often, though, women describe the act of *being* penetrated by another's tongue as potentially disturbing. The feeling described is one of being devoured, choked, or suffocated. It is as if somehow someone else's tongue represents, more than anything else, their desire to invade. Perhaps this is why kissing can sometimes feel like an act of resistance, a resistance to being invaded by another person. If kissing can provoke such sensations, it is hardly surprising that kissing should be the first sexual activity to show problems in a relationship.

The evidence that women more frequently shut their eyes during kissing also sheds interesting light on anxieties relating to kissing. Is it to do with the power that resides in the male look? Is it that women are unused to assuming the position of power which is involved in staring closely at another's eyes? Or is it also connected with the fear of penetration, as if the eyes, like the tongue, could also penetrate and invade? Perhaps the combination of the power of the look and the invasion by the tongue is too awesome, making one too vulnerable to the other's voracious intentions.

None of this is to suggest that women are not capable of enjoying kissing. Far from it. Kissing is probably for women the most sensational activity, representing the height of erotic involvement. Precisely because of its transgressive nature, crossing boundaries between people, engaging sensations usually kept at bay, kissing clearly produces 'excitement'. And sexual excitement in our culture does seem to have very close links with transgression, with engaging hidden sensations, bringing an underground stream to the surface.

Women's contradictory feelings about kissing are revealing about the construction of the 'feminine' position in our culture. The contradictory feelings are very likely produced because the oral sensations connected with kissing are so directly reminiscent of infantile sensual pleasures. Oral gratification is one of the earliest manifestations of infantile sexuality. More than just the satisfaction of hunger, the child enjoys the sensual pleasure of sucking and the physical sensations of warmth and closeness to another body. Kissing is the activity (eating aside), which most closely evokes all the oral sensations of that early infantile sexuality.

In a society which is predominantly heterosexual, the boy and girl have different relations to oral stimulation. As child care is currently practised in this society, the usual object of oral interest is the mother's breast. But as the child becomes more separate, the mother's breast is withdrawn and indeed becomes forbidden as an object of sensual interest. Both boy and girl child have to learn this. But for the girl, giving up the mother's breast is a permanent exile. The girl child is compelled to repress for ever the sensational pleasures connected with this dependent state of infancy, whereas the boy merely has to put them in abeyance. The breast, always an ambivalent object, becomes dangerous. And for the girl, oral sensations become problematic. The girl has to transfer her desire to incorporate another's body to the vagina away from the mouth, in order to take up a classically feminine position in a heterosexist society. The fantasy of being devoured by the mother as retribution for the child's own desire to introject the mother becomes more acute. This is not only because the mother's body is lost, but also because the desire for it is rendered guilt-laden.

Perhaps this is why penetration by the tongue may seem more awesome to women. Divorced from eating, kissing is a sensation directly evoking the sexual aspects of oral stimulation. Could it be that women fear they will be devoured, because memories are stirred up of this infantile fear of retribution for oral activities?

No wonder the kiss has come to be a most powerful erotic symbol in our culture. The second before the lips touch and the mouths open is the second before people's separation is destroyed and a whole series of physical sensations are activated. The minutest space between the lips stands as a magic metaphor for tactile, oral and nasal sensations that have been in abeyance since childhood. But as sexual relations are lived in this society, the kiss can become a source of anxiety. Because women learn to be in exile from those early physical sensations, when they are evoked in 'adult' relations it can be fearful. Being the most intimate and regressive of sensations, kissing is also most likely to evoke the fear of being destroyed and devoured.

Naughty but Nice:
Food Pornography

Have yet another bite at the cherry.

Naughty but nice

There's a full-page spread in a woman's magazine. It's captioned Breakfast Special, and shows a picture of every delicious breakfast imaginable. The hungry eye can delight in croissants with butter, exquisitely prepared bacon and eggs, toasted waffles with maple syrup. But over the top of the pictures there's a sinister message: 430 calories for the croissants; 300 for the waffles. The English breakfast takes the biscuit with a top score of 665 calories. It must be a galling sight for the readers of this particular magazine. Because it's *Slimmer* magazine. And one presumes the reader looks on these pleasures in the full knowledge that they had better not be indulged.

This pleasure in looking at the supposedly forbidden is reminiscent of another form of guilty-but-indulgent looking, that of sexual pornography. Sexual pornography as a separate realm of imagery exists because our society defines some explicit pictures of sexual activity or sexual parts as 'naughty', 'illicit'. These images are then made widely available through a massive and massively profitable industry.

The glossy pictures in slimming magazines show in glorious Technicolor all the illicit desires which make us fat. Many of the articles show almost life-size pictures of the real baddies of the dieting world – bags of crisps, peanuts, bars of chocolate, cream puddings. Diet foods are advertised as sensuously as possible. The food is made as appetizing as possible, often with explicit sexual references: 'Tip Top. For Girls who used to say No': 'Grapefruits. The Least Forbidden Fruit'.

Pictures in slimming magazines and those circulated around the slimming culture are only the hard core of food pictures which are in general circulation in women's magazines. Most women's magazines carry articles about food, recipes or advertising. All are accompanied by larger-than-life, elaborate pictures of food, cross-sections through a cream and strawberry sponge, or close-ups of succulent Orange and Walnut Roast Beef. Recipe books often dwell on the visual impact of food. Robert Carrier has glossy cards showing the dish in question and carrying the recipe on the back – just the right size for the pocket. In the street, billboards confront us with gargantuan cream cakes.

But it is only the unfortunate readers of the slimming magazines who are supposed to use the pictures as a substitute for the real thing. While other forms of food photography are meant to stimulate the desire to prepare and eat the food, for the slimmers it is a matter of feasting the eyes only.

Like sexual pornography, pictures of food provide a photographic genre geared towards one sex. And like sexual pornography, it is a regime of 'pleasure' which is incomprehensible to the opposite sex. This is because these pornographies are creating and indulging 'pleasures' which confirm or trap men and women in their respective positions of power and subordination.

Sexual pornography is an industry dealing in images geared towards men. Sexual pornography is dominated by pictures of women. It shows bits of women's bodies, women engaged in sex acts, women masturbating, women supposedly having orgasms. When the women look at the camera, it is with an expression of sexual arousal, interest and availability. The way in which women are posed for these images presupposes a male viewer, behind the camera, as it were, about to move in on the act.

Pornography is only the extreme end of how images of women are circulated in general in this society. Pornography is defined as being illicit, naughty, unacceptable for public display (though definitions of what is acceptable vary from one epoch to the next). It shows things which generally available images don't – penetration, masturbation, women's genitals. The porn industry then thrives on marketing and circulating these 'illicit' images. But if pornography is meant to be illicit, and hidden, the kinds of images it shows differ little from the more routinely available images of women. Page three nudes in daily papers, advertisements showing women, the representation of sex in non-pornographic films, all draw on the conventions by which women are represented in pornography. Women are made to look into the camera in the same way, their bodies are arranged in the same way, the same glossy photographic techniques are used, there is the same fragmentation of women's bodies, and a concomitant fetishistic concentration on bits of the body.

Many women now think that the way male arousal is catered for in these images is a problem. These images feed a belief that men have depersonalized sexual needs, like sleeping or going to the lavatory. Pornography as it is currently practised suggests that women's bodies are available to meet those needs. Men often say that porn is just fantasy, a harmless way of having pleasure as a substitute for the real thing. But women have begun to question this use of the term 'pleasure'. After all, the pleasure seems conditional on feeling power to use women's bodies. And maybe there's only a thin line between the fantasy and the lived experience of sexuality where men do sometimes force their sexual attentions on women.

If sexual pornography is a display of images which confirm men's sense of themselves as having power over women, food pornography is a regime of pleasurable images which has the opposite effect on its viewers – women. It indulges a pleasure which is linked to servitude and therefore confirms the subordinate position of women. Unlike sexual pornography, however, food porn cannot even be used without guilt. Because of pressures to diet, women have been made to feel guilty about enjoying food.

The use of food pornography is surprisingly widespread. All the women I have talked to about food have confessed to enjoying it. Few activities it seems rival relaxing in bed with a good recipe book. Some indulged in full colour pictures of gleaming bodies of Cold Mackerel Basquaise lying invitingly on a bed of peppers, or perfectly formed chocolate mousse topped with mounds of cream. The intellectuals expressed a preference for erotica, Elizabeth David's historical and literary titillation. All of us used the recipe books as aids to oral gratification, stimulants to imagine new combinations of food, ideas for producing a lovely meal.

Cooking food and presenting it beautifully is an act of servitude. It is a way of expressing affection through a gift. In fact, the preparation of a meal involves intensive domestic labour, the most devalued labour in this society. That we should aspire to produce perfectly finished and presented food is a symbol of a willing and enjoyable participation in servicing other people.

Food pornography exactly sustains these meanings relating to the preparation of food. The kinds of pictures used always repress the process of production of a meal. They are always beautifully lit, often touched up. The settings are invariably exquisite – a conservatory in the background, fresh flowers on the table. The dishes are expensive and look barely used.

There's a whole professional ideology connected with food photography. The *Focal Encyclopaedia of Photography* tells us that in a 'good food picture', 'the food must be both perfectly cooked and perfectly displayed' if it is to appeal to the magazine reader. The photographer 'must decide in advance on the correct style and arrangement of table linen, silver, china, flowers. Close attention to such details is vital because the final pictures must survive the critical inspection of housewives and cooks.' Food photographers are

supposed to be at the service of the expert chef, but sometimes
'the photographer learns by experience that certain foodstuffs do not
photograph well'. And in such circumstances, 'he must be able to
suggest reasonable substitutes'. Glycerine-covered green paper is a
well-known substitute for lettuce, which wilts under the bright lights
of a studio. And fast-melting foods like ice-cream pose interesting
technical problems for the food photographer. Occasionally, they do
get caught out – I recently saw a picture of a sausage dinner where a
nail was clearly visible, holding the sausage to its surroundings!
Virtually all meals shown in these photos are actually inedible. If
not actually made of plaster, most are sprayed or treated for
photographing. How ironic to think of the perfect meal destined for
the dustbin.

Food photographs are the culinary equivalent of the removal of
unsightly hairs. Not only do hours of work go into the preparation of
the settings and the dishes, but the finished photos are touched up
and imperfections removed to make the food look succulent and
glistening. The aim of these photos is the display of the perfect meal
in isolation from the kitchen context and the process of its production. There are no traces of the hours of shopping, cleaning, cutting
up, preparing, tidying up, arranging the table and the room which
in fact go into the production of a meal. Just as we know that
glamorous models in the adverts don't really look as they appear, so
we know perfectly well about the hours of untidy chaos involved in
the preparation of a meal. We know that photos of glamour models
are touched up, skin blemishes removed, excess fat literally cut out
of the picture. And – subconsciously at least – we probably realize
the same process has been at work on the Black Forest Gâteau. But
the ideal images still linger in our minds as a lure. A meal should
really look like the pictures. And that's how the images produce
complicity in our subordination. We aim at giving others pleasure
by obliterating the traces of our labour.

But it is not as if, even if we could produce this perfect meal, we
could wholeheartedly enjoy it. Because at the same time as food is
presented as the one legitimate sensual pleasure for women we are
simultaneously told that women shouldn't eat too much. Food is
Naughty but Nice, as the current Real Dairy Cream advertisement
announces.

This guilt connected with eating has become severe over the last
few decades. It's a result of the growing pressure over these years
towards the ideal shape of women. This shape – discussed in 'The

Body Beautiful' (see page 37) – is more like an adolescent than a woman, a silhouette rather than a soft body. There's a current dictum in slimming circles: 'If you can pinch an inch, you may need to lose weight.' This seems a particularly vicious control of female contours in a society obsessed with eating and uninterested in physical exertion. Dieting is the forcible imposition of an ideal shape on a woman's body.

The presentation of food sets up a particular trap for women. The glossy, sensual photography legitimates oral desires and pleasures for women in a way that sexual interest for women is never legitimated. At the same time, however, much of the food photography constructs a direct equation between food and fat, an equation which can only generate guilt about oral pleasures. Look at the way advertising presents food, drawing a direct equation between what women eat and what shape they will be. Tab is the low-calorie drink from Coca-Cola. Its advertising campaign shows a glass of the stuff which is in the shape of a woman's body! Beside the glass are the statistics 35″ 22″ 35″. A Sweetex advertisement shows two slender women and exhorts 'Take the lumps out of your life. Take Sweetex'! Heinz promotes its 'Slimway Mayonnaise' with a picture of a very lurid lobster and the caption 'Mayonnaise without guilt'. Tea even 'adds a little weight to the slimming argument'. Another soft-drink company exhorts: 'Spoil yourself, not your figure', which is a common promise for slimming foods. Nor is this phenomenon confined to slimming foods. Women's magazines have articles about whether 'your taste buds are ruining your figure', and creamy foods are offered as wicked but worth it.

An equation is set up in this kind of writing and these pictures between what goes into the mouth and the shape your body will be. It is as if we swallow a mouthful and it goes immediately, without digestion, to join the 'cellulite'. If we give this a moment's thought, we realize it is nonsense. There's no direct correlation between food into the mouth and fat; that's about the *only* thing on which all the diet experts agree. People have different metabolisms, use food differently. Different things in different people's lives affect what they eat and what effect that eating has on overall health. But the simplistic ideologies behind food and dieting cultures reinforce the guilt associated with food for women. Oral pleasures are only really permissible when tied to the servicing of others in the production of a meal. Women are controlled and punished if they indulge themselves.

The way images of food are made and circulated is not just an innocent catering for pleasures. They also meddle in people's sense of themselves and their self-worth. In a sexually divided and hierarchical society, these pleasures are tied to positions of power and subordination.

Let's have a meal together

When 800 million people in the world live under the constant threat of starvation, it may seem frivolous to look at meals in terms of sexual politics. But *how* food is consumed and prepared has crucial implications for women in this society, because it expresses deeply held ideologies of provision and dependency. Where eating is no longer a matter of absolute survival, the preparation and contexts of food are laced with social symbolism. Eating appears to be utterly natural – like breathing, an essential part of our survival. So it is hard to imagine that along with the nourishment we might be swallowing a whole lot more besides. (And I'm not referring to the chemical additives.) This very appearance of naturalness disguises the fact that women's surbordination is expressed in the ways we eat. Who does the cooking, what is served up in what order by whom and in what settings are all practices determined by the social significance they have.

In spite of the general level of affluence in Western society, eating is not a particularly easy business. As a society we are plagued with alimentary disorders and neuroses connected with eating – ulcers, indigestion, anorexia, bulimia. Women, in particular, sometimes find eating in public very difficult since there's too much anxiety connected with social eating. These disorders and neuroses connected with food surely reflect on the indigestible aspects of social and sexual symbolism associated with eating.

Just take the classic example of when a man says, 'Let's have a meal together sometime.' Only in recent times, with the impact of feminist ideologies, have women been able to establish the possibility of paying for their own meal, and the traditional practice is by no means dead. The bill is still presented to the man, the man is invited to taste the wines, and some extremely smart (and reactionary) restaurants give women a menu without prices.

Some cite this as a typical example of the triviality of feminism's concerns, but such a battle, small though it may seem, was necessary to combat the symbolism behind accepting a meal from a man. Lurking behind such a treat is the symbolism of the business man–client relationship. In this relationship, a meal is provided by the business or company seeking the services of a particular person. The 'meal out' in a good restaurant is paid for by the company as a way of expressing the wealth, status and power of the business. The meal impresses the client and invariably puts him in a relationship of obligation. The symbolism between men and women to some extent reproduces this symbolism, the symbolism of the male provider. What is demonstrated is the ability to provide, and economic status in the world. In addition these 'traditional' meals eaten out by a man and woman carry meanings not dissimilar from those pertaining to prostitution. Services are bought for a fee. In routine sexual relations, services are expected in return for provision. Small wonder that even the most impoverished women sometimes make an issue about paying for themselves just in case unwanted sexual attentions should be wheeled in after the starters.

A close scrutiny of the average restaurant shows that even the lay-out seems designed to affirm the symbolism of business man–client relationship, whether it is between the sexes or between companies. The only people who can afford to eat out are either people with expense accounts or those who do so for special occasions. Restaurants always seem to be packed with business men doing deals or row after row of heterosexual couples. Locked in intense dialogue (propositions or arguments) or staring at each other in stony silence, you might get the impression visiting the average restaurant for the first time that no other relationship existed under the sun. (And that this wasn't good news.) This is quite different from other societies, such as the Chinese, where eating out is habitual, and eating with any less than ten people decidedly odd. Restaurants in our society, however, seem to reinforce the impression that special-occasion meals are more often than not symbolic affirmations of relations of power and obligations.

Most of our eating anxieties start earlier than the days of 'special occasions' in restaurants. Eating neuroses usually stem from the early experiences of family eating, from the unspoken conflicts and turbulent emotions associated with family meals. No less than eating out, though, family meals are redolent with the symbolism of economic provision and dependency.

Everyone has stories of family meals ending in some kind of drama or chaos. Either violent arguments break out – food hits the floor, drink is hurled across the room, joints grow cold as insults rise in a crescendo, mothers and children silently weep into their congealing food – or sometimes an embarrassing and hostile silence descends, no one daring risk further misunderstanding.

Eating a meal together in the family is burdened with the heavy symbolism of provision and dependency. This becomes most apparent in the big communal meals – the Sunday lunch and the

Christmas dinner. Indeed, Christmas in a secular society is a festivity primarily concerned with eating and, as such, highlights the politics of eating.

There are two major rituals associated with Christmas, that of present-giving and that of excessive eating. Both are rituals which crop up in numerous societies, expressing the ability to provide and mutual dependency. Present-giving, for example, is a way of expressing people's dependency on one another, people's need for each other. The mutal exchange of gifts is designed to establish a sense of reciprocity and to quell anxieties about the separateness of other people. They need you as much as you need them.

Mutual present-giving has been well documented in anthropology[1] and is seen by many as a fundamental ritual of any human society by which *social* bonds are recognized. By social I mean the dependency of individuals on the group, the inability of an individual to survive without social ties and obligations. Festive eating equally signifies an affirmation of the survival of society. The essence of a feast is that it should be excessive, that it should involve quantities and types of foods not normally eaten, in order to signify profusion and survival. These connotations have certainly been carried over into our secular winter festival.

The criterion by which a Christmas dinner is judged successful is the extent to which it defeats the eater. What is noted is the enormous size of the turkey, the number of mince pies consumed. Even falling into an unconscious stupor acquires a certain glamour, the culmination of the curious pattern of Christmas eating – intensive preparation, high expectations, exchange, indulgence, anticlimax, sleep. Even the food combinations are transgressive. Sweet foods and savoury are combined in ways which are on the whole confined to Christmas meals – jam with meat, fruit and savouries in puddings, and so on.

But analysis of meals and present-giving doesn't just reveal two universal practices where people mutually express dependency and everything is egalitarian and unproblematic. Providing the feast, and even giving the most spectacular presents, are also ways of expressing power. Food in hierarchical societies is often appropriated and controlled. Giving food out in feasts is a way in which hierarchical positions are demonstrated.

In a documentary about the Ashanti, a matrilineal society in

[1] See, for example M. Mauss, *The Gift*, Routledge, London, 1970.

Africa, a group of men were asked whether they ever did the cooking.[2] Their response was one of amazement: 'Men, cook? What an extraordinary idea! Men do not worship women so why should men serve food? Women worship men – they cook food for us.' This shocked response is symptomatic of the fact that in many societies – though not all – the preparation of food is considered an act of servitude, the demonstration of a subordinate and servicing social position.

Our Western hierarchical society contains many of these elements. It is women who prepare the food and both Sunday lunches and Christmas dinner require intensive labour. Yet when it comes to serving the food, it is traditionally the male role to carve the meat and pass the plates around. These ritual meals are designed to signify the ability of men to provide and the duty of women to prepare and service.

There are additional connotations in our symbolic meals. For these symbolic meals are confined to a small nuclear family. Present-giving between friends is by no means obligatory, whereas a forgotten relative is likely to engender terrible guilt. Ritual eating as well is a symbolic activity which sits oddly on groups when taken outside the family. There's a rush *not* to carve, an embarrassment about laying on a joint just for convention's sake.

The rituals of mutual present-giving and symbolic eating as practised in our society mean that social dependency is symbolized almost exclusively within the family. The festival of Christmas expresses the idea that the restricted family can provide materially and exclusively for all our needs. On the table are the visible signs of the family's ability to provide. The meal is the product of woman's domestic labour, demonstrating her willingness to serve the family and expressing her love through the preparation of food. The man carves, taking up his role as economic provider.

The alimentary disorders which rack our society may well be the physical expression of the limitations of an ideology which claims that a small family can provide for all our needs. Family festivities can be a real gut-bomb, because along with the food go complex feelings of inadequacy, disappointment and guilt. Expecting too much from too few is a certain recipe for disaster, and all the members of the family are likely to suffer. Because the symbolism suggests that the family can provide everything, family members feel

[2] 'Ashanti Market Women'. *Disappearing World* series for Granada TV, directed by Claudia Milne.

guilt if they express a need for emotional support from outsiders. This need is sometimes experienced as guilt for rejecting the family's love, when it is merely recognizing more extensive social needs that can't always be met in the family.

The attempt to make the family the place where all the material and emotional support can be supplied has been particularly exacting for women. Women, if confined to the home, often become isolated. In these circumstances, often for practical reasons like child care, there's no escape route like work, and women find themselves more subject to emotional investment in the family. In the current situation, it is an investment bound for disappointment, since it is not shared by men.

Social changes in living arrangements over the last few decades are fair evidence of the limitations of the nuclear family.[3] Divorce has doubled in the last ten years and the number of single-parent families has increased enormously. Many people are opting for different kinds of living arrangements. And women have become vociferously critical of the ideology of male provision, an ideology which feeds back into an economy where women are ghettoized in low-paid jobs. It is also an ideology used to excuse all kinds of aggressive and uncaring behaviour in the home.

Eating meals is a hazardous activity, infused as it is with implications for sex roles and living arrangements. Small wonder that our digestive tracts have become the site of hidden warfare.

[3] For a summary of household patterns, see The Study Commission on the Family, *Families in the Future*, 1983. For an examination of how the traditional family affects women, see L. Segal (ed.), *What is to be Done About the Family?*, Penguin, 1983, especially the article by F. Bennett which discusses the relationship between the state and women's economic dependency within the family.

The Mouth

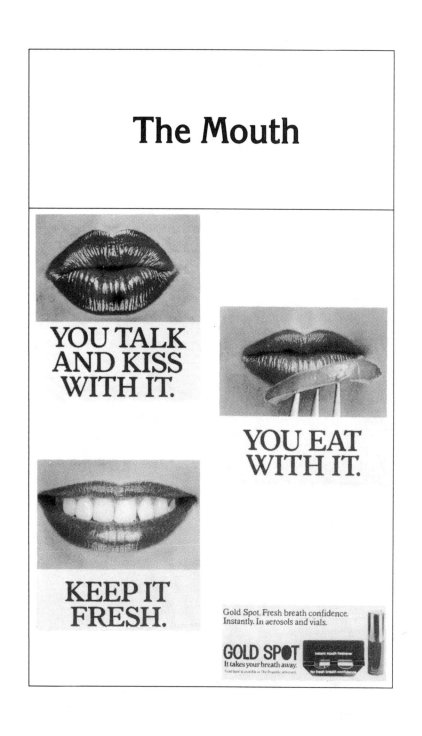

YOU TALK AND KISS WITH IT.

YOU EAT WITH IT.

KEEP IT FRESH.

Of all the sensations, visual impressions take pride of place in this society. The representations of sexuality which surround us – be they visual images or writings about sex – all seem to stress that the eyes are the most important sex organs. But possibly because visual stimulation is so tied to men's scrutiny of women, it doesn't seem to offer women the same delights. Faced with explanations about the visual basis for sexual attraction, pleasure through the eyes, women continue to hold other sensations just as dear. And the mouth seems to be the organ where some of the most intense sensations are located.

Actually, the mouth seems to be women's most intimate orifice, often represented as the most personal aspect of self. Source of gratifications, illicit and delicious intimacies, the organ of confession, the mouth is strangely crossed by the structures of eroticism *and* prohibition which touch on women in this society. Is this an explanation for the fashion of lipstick? For centuries, women have painted their lips in a sort of brash advertisement for the pleasures of the oral zone. Yet as Angela Carter has noted, the colour most usual for this advertisement is red, like blood: 'We are so used to the bright red mouth we no longer see it as the wound it mimics, except in the treacherous lucidity of paranoia. Now the mouth is back as a bloody gash, a visible wound. This mouth bleeds over everything, cups, ice-cream, table napkins, towels.'[1] Is it that in this combination of loud advertisement and the colour of blood, lipstick has condensed the eroticisms and the prohibitions around the mouth? For blood on a woman's orifice reminds me of another orifice which bleeds. Is it that women can advertise their oral appetite only if at the same time they acknowledge a prohibition – that incorporation has now been properly transferred to the vagina?

The mouth and its surroundings can evidently be the site of sensual and sexual pleasures for both men and women. In fact, psychoanalysis has suggested that the oral phase is the very first phase in the sexual life of all human beings.[2] General sexual drives and aims, it is suggested, arise at first attached to the vital function of feeding. Later, these drives and aims become detached, erotic

[1] Angela Carter, *Nothing Sacred*, Virago, 1982.
[2] In 1915, Freud described the oral stage as the first stage of sexual life. The source is the oral zone; the object is closely associated with that of the ingestion of food; the aim is incorporation. See Freud, Standard Edition, Vol. VII, p. 198.

pleasures in their own right. In principle, then, this happens to both male and female; at first stimulated by the ingestion of food, the mouth becomes a source of erotic pleasure in its own right.

Actually, as sexuality is currently lived, the sensations connected with the mouth are experienced differently by men and women. Sensations surrounding the mouth create at least equal proportions of pleasure and anxiety for women. Men, on the other hand, can follow their oral cravings in relatively uncomplicated ways. Indeed, much of men's social life could be seen as a collective celebration of oral pleasures. Drinking bouts, eating hearty meals, smoking (only comparatively recently acceptable for women), talking and shouting in public, at football matches, along the streets. All these uses of the mouth characterize the ways in which men seem to enjoy being with each other.

But for women, it is a very different story. Complicated taboos and prohibitions surround the sensual pleasures of the mouth. In fact, the mouth appears to be the organ where the tightest controls are placed on women's behaviour, where women's sensual life is most closely policed. No one is in any doubt about the strengths of women's oral appetites. Food, kissing, verbal foreplay – these are some of the great delights of female erotic life. But all the evidence suggests that these pursuits can quickly become problematic. When oral pleasures are indulged, there's often a whole train of guilty and anxious consequences to deal with.

The mouth probably inhabits this complicated place in women's sensual life for two reasons. First, it is through the mouth, in speaking, that a person asserts her presence in the world. And second, because the mouth is so crucially connected with eating and nurturing, oral pleasures bring women into direct confrontation with ideologies about women's appetites, and women's domestic place.

While the mouth can be used to establish a person's presence in the world, it is obvious that this is no easy task for women. Men silence women's speech in public. It is men's speech and volume which dominates the public domain; women's comments are often rendered marginal or irrelevant (see also 'The Voice' p.151). With such control exercised over women's ability to represent themselves, there's no surprise to find that when women *do* speak in public and establish their needs, a terrible guilt often ensues. It seems that we have internalized effectively the repression of our speech; when we speak it can feel as if we have no right to do so, that we are unworthy of expressing our needs.

No such doubts beset men. The public domain is noisy with men's speech; mostly assertive and often belligerent. No equivalent grip of guilt seems to tighten round men's throats. Guilt, of course, is always a sign that what has been expressed or thought is felt to be unacceptable. This guilt is a sign that, as women, we have internalized the external constraints on our speech. There are pressing parallels with the guilt which women also feel about eating, a guilt that we have overstepped our rightful position in the world and are about to acquire a body that will publicize this fact.

Oral pursuits, then, can be assertive when they are expressed in speech. The other principal area of anxiety and guilt for women concerns the mouth as the site of consumption, of introjection. The fare fed to us about dieting is so powerful because it plays on these anxieties as well as on visual ones about ideal shape. In this society, it is women who provide the satisfaction for the oral desires of others, be they men or children. Like the pelican of the medieval bestiary, it is women who dole out their lifeblood for their offspring. Nowadays we know that the pelicans aren't ripping out their own breasts but are regurgitating food for their young, just as we've found more subtle ways of ensuring that women give, provide nourishment, rather than take and ingest nourishment for themselves. There's a common fantasy among women that they might be destroyed for the guilty and greedy desires they felt towards their mothers. And this fantasy has a material basis in this society, for domestic relations and relations between the sexes are lived out in ways which put women in danger of being destroyed or consumed; domestic relations are ordered around the satisfaction of men's and children's oral needs. Women are expected to nourish not to demand.

The control of the pleasures of the mouth is particularly fierce when it concerns women's position as mothers. Here, more than anywhere else, anxieties about food, feeding and provision have been intensified by ideologies controlling the social situation of women. These ideologies are focused on the question of 'adequate' mothering. Mothers are asked whether children are adequately nourished, and increasingly, whether children are accepting this maternal nourishment.

The activity of feeding and rearing babies has been made the object of intensive medical and state intervention over the last hundred years. Numerous talks and classes have been given; endless pamphlets and books published. The mother–child relationship has become the object of intensive scrutiny by the state.[3] And the state doesn't stop at just keeping an eye on how things are going. There's the threat of forcible intervention; if a mother fails the child will be taken away into care. The first forms of intervention in the mother–child relationship were primarily concerned with feeding and the physical well-being of the child, a concern which emerged after the discovery of mass undernourishment at the time of the First World War. Since the Second World War, another series of concerns have come to the fore. As well as the necessary vitamins and protein, the state watches closely whether the child is getting a well-balanced diet of motherly love, discipline and heterosexual normality. Visitors call, keeping a benign check on the child's hearing and the emotional temperature of its surroundings. Woe to the mother who is caught by the Health Visitor when her son is wearing her daughter's dress, as happened to a friend of mine. Explanations concerning the washing were not accepted; from then on the home was tightly scrutinized.

This is about the only time in our lifespan that the state and, therefore, medical provision pay attention to the health of the citizen. Normally, illness is only the concern of the state when it becomes critical, or if it claims attention as a valid research subject. There are lamentably few forms of preventive medicine.

For the mother–child relationship, however, there's a whole battery of advice and help. Maybe it is not of the kind women would want, but there it is, watching over what the mother is up to. Indeed, it is not far fetched to suggest that, through the mother–child relationship, the state has access to our homes. The mother–child relationship is the way by which the domestic is scrutinized.

Since the end of the last century, the British state has taken an increasing interest in the hygiene – sexual and medical – of the citizen's body. But this attention has been focused almost exclusively on the mother–child relationship. The state conducts its researches and offers moral guidance only within the confines of the family. This concern with the physical, emotional and sexual well-being of the future citizen has had a particular effect on women. There can be no doubt that the concern has created an additional burden on women as mothers, since a distinct ideology of 'adequate' mothering has been constructed. Above and beyond giving birth

[3] For an account of the relations between the state and mothering in the twentieth century, see D. Riley, *War in the Nursery*, 'Theories of the Child and Mother', Virago, 1983.

and feeding as adequately as possible with limited resources, women are now subject to endless anxieties about whether they are 'mothering' properly. Are they touching the child too much, or too little, in the wrong way or in the wrong places? Are women saying too much to their children or too little? Is the food nourishing enough or too rich? What does the child's acceptance or rejection of the food signify? Overprotective mothering? Inadequate love? These pronouncements on adequate mothering are so strong they even have the power to infect retrospectively. Older women, who were not subjected to the same language, are now asking themselves how they fared. 'If I'd have known how much was at stake, I'd have been more careful' – such is the voice of the retrospective guilt engendered by the terrific force of criticism which is currently directed at mothers.

The growing child and its health has become a veritable machine whose function, provisions, exercise and emotional temperature must be precisely observed and regulated. Any illness, rebellion, or rejection of food becomes a source of discussion about the mother's failure. Only by being extraordinarily strong can women resist these enquiries and establish their personal autonomy. Only by making difficult decisions can women evade the total exhaustion engendered by this scrutiny and get on with their lives.

It is not surprising that every mouthful the child takes has become a measure by which the adequacy of mothering can be assessed. Around the child's feeding, a whole drama is played out around which the adequacy of maternal provision can be assessed. And this anxiety, produced by medical and scientific opinion, overlays the already anxious relations which a mother and child will have on the subject of food. Such opinion crosses over the unconscious conflicts which a woman experiences between the command to provide, to give out and nourish, and the fear that, in so doing, she may be consumed and disappear altogether.

Taking something in through the mouth is evidently a sensation closely connected in our minds and our emotions with survival. Because of feeding and nourishing, oral gratification is a sensation closely associated with making claims on the world, asserting a right to exist and a need for provision. But women quickly learn that they cannot *take* from the world, can't assert their needs in quite that way. For this reason, the sensual pleasures of the mouth don't have the same place in men's lives as they do in women's. Sexual relations are arranged in our society in such a way that men can take pleasure from the world into their mouths. Indeed, it is often men's infantile oral needs which are sustained in an adult heterosexual relationship. But for women the pursuit of oral pleasure runs up against prohibitions and controls, against social prescriptions about feeding and food, against cultural prescriptions about women's appetite and women's duty to give out. The mouth for women is a site of drama, a drama between the desire to pursue active needs and against the prohibitions levelled against women's behaviour. When women attempt to lay claim to the pleasures of the mouth, they are often constricted by anxiety about transgressing the appropriate expression of female desire.

PART III

THE VOICE

What is this thing between us?

The language of love undoubtedly changes through the course of history. And the metaphors, similes and technical vocabulary used to describe the emotions of love tell us a great deal about the values current in society. It is hard to imagine, except perhaps in a Georgette Heyer novel, anyone describing their love affair in the following terms: 'Att those times my effections ran out violently after her, so that I was never contented one day to an end unless I had seene her and chiefly my effections were set upon her virtues and womenly qualities.' But these are the words used by a certain Roger Lowe who kept records of his numerous loves between the years 1663 and 1674.[1]

We don't hear much talk these days of affections, virtues or womanly qualities. What we do hear a lot about, though, is relationships – 'good relationships', 'bad relationships', 'compatible relationships', 'committed relationships'. A relationship can be 'calm' and 'caring', 'mutually supportive', or 'devastating'. What we have here is a whole technical vocabulary of 'the relationship', detailing the complicated dynamic between two people *and* all their 'previous involvements' as well.

The relationship is a sort of Frankenstein's monster. Spawned by the pseudo-scientists, it has taken on a life of its own, to the extent that instead of two characters, every love affair now involves three. People of the class and educational background who use this language don't fall in love with each other or become attracted to personal qualities. Instead they have a complicated initiation into a whole technical vocabulary of the emotions. Along with having sex with someone, we have to expect to become familiar with their 'complexes'; we have to watch out for 'projections', 'defensiveness' and 'possessiveness'. We have to expect 'to negotiate' degrees of 'dependence', and 'independence'; and we have to be prepared for 'conflict' or 'hassle' before any 'security' is achieved.

Language conditions what we think and indeed delineates the possibilities for what we feel about circumstances and events. So the enactment of desire is really experienced in these terms. Relationships have their own dynamic based on the difference between how two people behave with each other, and how they behave with other people. In such a context behaviour is not seen as good or bad,

[1] *Diary of Roger Lowe*, ed W. L. Sachse, London, 1938.

responsible or irresponsible. Instead, the behaviour is judged in terms of how it affects the relationship.

This new space of the emotional life, known as 'the relationship', appears to be the absolute aim of certain social groupings. Be it calm or stormy, destructive or supportive, the relationship is an aim in itself. Everywhere you look, you see 'the relationship' upheld as a most desirable state. And 'lack of relationship' is a state to be pitied, the state that makes for 'problems'. One of the popular sexology journals, *Man and Woman*, made this pleasingly explicit in its propaganda. The journal, it announced, was 'for people with relationships not problems'. Yet there are some rather strange aspects to the language of 'the relationship' as it is currently spoken. These strange aspects alert us to the fact that all is not well between the sexes. For the dominant metaphors in which relationships are described are the metaphors of the stock-exchange and of war.

The language of the emotions bears startling resemblances to descriptions of the economic activities of the capitalist system. It describes losses, gains, outlays, investments and returns. And it is, in essence, aggressive. Take the very goal of a *committed* relationship. The ultimate goal is *security* and *trust*, two specifically capitalist modes of holding property. The greatest disaster for a relationship is *loss*, a *wasted* effort. We talk of *commitments* to one another, we take *risks* that don't *pay off*; we seek *assurance* from one another. If we are fortunate, we have a *rewarding* relationship. Personal behaviour, too, is described in these terms. Protagonists are accused of being *possessive* or *dependent*, and are praised for being *self-sufficient*.

This is the language of economic competition and survival. Implicitly, it refers to the issue of who will support whom, who is dependent on whom, who owns the other person. It speaks of a desire to profit from experience, of a desire to have material gains, and of the economic base line of sexual relations. The aggression implicit in the language is obvious. It speaks of a system where dog eats dog and only a few succeed. But the aggression implied here is mild compared with the other great metaphor for emotional life, that of warfare. Protagonists in a relationship can be described as *triumphant*, *victorious*, or *defeated*. We talk of *peaceful* or *destructive* or *devastating* experiences. We talk of people *surrendering*, or *resisting*, or behaving *defensively*. Relationships are described as being *dangerous* or *explosive*. *Reconciliations* or *truces* are sometimes achieved between the *warring* forces. And if that happens we call ourselves *survivors*.

The underlying message of competition and aggression is striking in both these metaphors, suggesting that there's more at work than a simple increase in technical vocabulary. Here is the ultimate aim of our society, the relationship, described in terms redolent of hostility, competition and aggression. And the terms are drawn from masculine activities, conflict and competition between individuals and nations.

It won't come as any surprise to the attentive reader that I think this language somehow touches quite perceptively on some of the elements which are actually at play in sexual relations. The questions for me are rather, how did this language arise, and does it really help us understand the structure of sexual relations?

The technical language of the relationship is a language which has filtered back from psychoanalytic and therapeutic interpretations of human behaviour. Pop sex psychology has made this kind of language widely available. Spilling off the couches it spread like an epidemic through the middle classes and has become the dominant way of understanding relationships. Freud was perhaps the first to uncover what he called 'unconscious thought', the existence of feelings and ideas which appeared to contradict or underlie in some complicated way our conscious thought. Psychoanalysis changed the whole way in which behaviour could be understood. Psychoanalytic discoveries of the unconscious were based on analytic practice – the investigation of past experiences, personal history and conflicts which lay behind the patient's current behaviour. It shouldn't really surprise us that this approach to relationships uncovered a whole battlefield where economic power and inter-sex competition conditioned the quality of emotional experience.

It is certainly the case that there is an objective basis to economic power within a relationship. And as with any situation of unequal power, we must expect to find resistance, guerrilla warfare and liberation struggles. The days may have gone when men were able to view their wives as possessions in the literal sense, but there is still a situation where men have economic power and privilege. Men are in general in higher-paid jobs; women are still largely confined to low-paid jobs and are still expected to service men and children. In such a situation, there are literal as well as metaphorical issues of dependence and independence.

There is still, for example, an ideology which dictates that a male wage should be a family wage. Consequently male employment tends to be better paid than traditionally 'female' jobs, like secretarial or nursing work. It is still almost invariably women who give up paid work to care for children, and, indeed, current state benefits perpetuate what is thought to be this desirable state of affairs. So, for example, if a man stays at home to look after the children and the working wife falls ill, she is not entitled to claim benefit for him as a dependant. Women, however, are regularly treated as dependants. The papers recently have been full of references to the psychological damage which unemployment causes men. Yet, for years, women have been far more vulnerable than men to the vicissitudes of the employment market. Women are called into the labour market when needed, as in times of war, then removed forcibly back into the home. The fact that women take the major responsibility for the lives of the future generation means that women can't expect an unbroken working life. In general, women must rely for at least some periods of their lives on male earnings or, failing this, on a small state benefit.

There is then a reality of economic dependency in most hetero-sexual relationships, and this sometimes has dire psychological consequences for women. Women feel guilty about stepping out of line, asserting their needs and not being good wives. And it is all too easy to lose a sense of identity when cut off from waged work, in a society where identity is so tied up with what work you do and how much you get paid, Dependency, economic security, self-sufficiency, independence and control are real issues in how the household is arranged in our society. It shouldn't be a surprise to find that when unconscious fears and needs are betrayed by the terms we use to discuss 'the relationship', they reflect the dangers endemic to the way that sexual relations are arranged.

Equally the issue of warfare is no less real. As men and women are currently formed, there are good reasons for sex antagonism. For a woman, a heterosexual relationship may mean being obscured by a man's identity and career, subordinating her personal needs to those of her children and husband. And because of the way in which men have been trained to pursue economic status and identity, and women have been trained to care for the home and interpersonal relation-ships, the sexes have developed very different ways of communicat-ing. Women must be caring, and communicative; men must be in control, strong, not weak and dependent. No wonder such a gulf exists between the sexes. No wonder there's such good cause for fear and antagonism. For women there are real reasons to fear lack of support but equally strong reasons to fear over-dependency. For men, there is a fear that through a relationship with a woman, certain powers will have to be abdicated.

With so much unconscious fear and antagonism, reflected in the language, it sometimes seems utterly unlikely that either sex should ever find consolation in the other. And were it not for the fact that women are remarkably good at subordinating their own active needs the whole system would probably break down. Heterosexual relations are fraught with real conflicts. There are fears that economic support will not be given and fears that economic resources will be drained; there are fears that if one person is self-reliant, the other will disappear.

But the way in which the language has passed into widespread use actually works to obscure these very structures. The metaphors touch on the real circumstances in which sexual relations are conducted, but they are misplaced. We do not normally recognize the basis of the metaphors, their origin in masculine activities – economic competition and military competition. Instead we use them as convenient terms to describe what is happening between two people. In these circumstances the metaphors are pulled out of their own context, and by the same token they can elevate the emotions out of the sphere of social relations. Emotions are treated in a vacuum. Conflicts, struggles, fear of dependency, destruction, rewards, all become the grisly and inevitable consequences of the human condition. Instead of a language sensitive to psychic structures *and* social conditions we are treated to tedious accounts of strife in the cortex, investments in the emotions.

The relationship monster has truly exceeded all expectations. Escaping from the laboratory of social conditions, it sets itself up as an alien, isolated from history and social relations. The only clue left that betrays the real basis of 'the relationship', like the bolt through the neck of Frankenstein's monster, is the kind of metaphor used to discuss the relationship. Talking about relationships has become a sort of game which consenting adults of a certain class can play. By becoming a thing in itself, the relationship mystifies the general social conditions behind the way emotional relations are lived out. And by becoming a game – a good hard game – it doesn't seem so important to deal with problems about sexual relations collectively. 'Relationship' is not a game for the whole of society; only two can play this game.

'Have you tried talking about it?'

Agony aunts go to some pains to insist that they don't offer advice in their advice columns. Agony aunts claim that they listen to what their readers have to say and hope that the letters suggest their own solutions. 'It would be arrogant for me to tell them what to do,' says Marjorie Proops of the *Daily Mirror* (quoted in *Miss London*, May 1977). Claire Rayner of the *Sun* likewise claims 'never to have solved anyone's problems but simply to have pointed people in the right direction' (ibid.). Irma Kurtz of *Cosmopolitan* goes further; advice, she writes, 'is the least important thing an advice column offers. The greatest good we do the individual is to give her the chance, possibly for the first time ever, to write her problem down and in writing it down to effect an alignment of thoughts that have been scattered by crisis' (*Guardian*, 28 September 1981).

Significantly, however, Irma Kurtz goes on to give an example of how an agony aunt will listen and hear what the letter-writer is really trying to say. Writers, she says, often betray, unbeknown to themselves, 'what the real problem is'. In doing so, they also point towards their own solution. 'Then all I need to do is point out to her a phrase she herself has used. "I cannot talk to my husband about this . . ." for example. "Never mind your lack of ardour, or your flat chest, or your extra-marital desires," I can then reply, "why can't you talk to your husband?"' (ibid.).

The example given by Irma Kurtz is not in fact as random as she'd have us suppose. Talking out your problems with your nearest and dearest is a primary solution offered by the advice columnists. And 'Have you tried talking about it?' is one of the most common questions asked by the agony aunts in response to the thousands of letters which women write to the problem pages of magazines. 'But do tell your father how you feel, won't you?' writes Virginia Ironside (*Woman*, May 1982), and in a different letter on the same page, she makes some suggestions about how to cope with a husband's impotence: '. . . maybe he has a deep-seated anxiety about the future of his life that he is not admitting to you or even to himself? Talk, talk and more talk would undoubtedly help you both. And I think you could certainly put your mixed feelings about the problem to him without making him feel less of a man.'

The incitement to talk continues across the pages of any number of different magazines. 'Never stop talking with him, discussing, rationalizing. Don't nurse your grievances silently. Be open and honest and ask the same of him' (Rose Shephard, *Honey*, October 1981). 'After you understand more, you will be able to talk to your husband calmly and then work out what you want to do' (Irma Kurtz, *Cosmopolitan*, February 1981). 'Talk to your parents rationally, tell them that you do love this young man and that the years you have shared with him prove it is not a mere infatuation' (ibid.). Confide, talk, tell all; above all, talk rationally and make him or them do the same.

This injunction to confide and tell all, to talk it through calmly is, after all, only an extension of the activity of the problem pages themselves. Advice columns are built on acts of public confession, of making your innermost thoughts and feelings known by telling the advice columnist what is happening to you. It is common to read or hear (on the now common radio advice phone-ins) the following statement: 'You have taken it this far in writing to me. Now take it further. Talk to your husband, your parent, a doctor, a marriage guidance counsellor, a psychotherapist. You have made a beginning, now talk some more.' Advice columns recently have become a sort of poor person's introduction to the world of professional therapy.

If telling it all in the pages of an advice column is just the beginning of the great verbal intercourse that will change the letter-writer's life, for the readers of the column, the letters are themselves the spectacle. It may be clear enough why the letters are written, but why are they printed, why do people delight in reading them when the problems are not often directly connected with their own? The act of writing it down, as much as being the start of therapeutic action for the writers, is also the basis of the spectacle. Problem pages are revelations by ordinary women, who are neither novelists nor journalists, about their personal lives. And the aspects of personal lives which fill up the columns are invariably connected with 'sexual problems'. 'Should I tell my parents' the letters ask; 'I don't want sex any more' or 'I'm having an affair with a married man' they confide. Some of the agony aunts describe these as the timeless human problems, the only changes being at what age women have to start grappling with these problems: 'Mary Grant finds that the timeless problems of loss of love and the search for it, marriage and courtship, the eternal problems based on human nature, have gone down the age scale in the last few years' (*Miss London*, op. cit.).

In fact, the centrality given to sexual and emotional problems as the most devastating problems of a woman's life is relatively recent. Women have been encouraged to write to magazines for a long time, asking for beauty or home advice; but it is only since the Second World War that they have been exhorted to reveal to all the intimate doings of their sex lives. Problem pages believe they are dealing with timeless human emotions. In fact, problem pages are themselves a historically specific symptom of the way in which sexuality and its emotional consequences have been catapulted to the foreground in our culture as the true expression of our most intimate selves.

Actually, the spectacle of the problem page is for the general magazine reader a distinct sub-genre of sexual fiction. It is not quite a novel, with the possibilities novels have for tracing minute reactions. It is more like the so-called journalism of tabloid newspapers such as the *Sun* or the *Star*. Here we get endless superficial short stories dealing with sexual intrigue, scandal and gossip about personalities. But newspaper stories are intensely normalizing. They present a world of little scandals, of wife-swapping, of adultery and murder, which is newsworthy precisely because it is supposed to be different from the way the average newspaper reader is supposed to live. It allows the reader to have a good look and feel comfortably different. Problem pages deal in a different matter. They are the stuff of intrigue – rejection, adultery, jealousy, impotence – but they are the intimate confessions of the protagonists. These letters are from women trying to deal with moral, sexual and emotional choices, revealing to the reader their internal dilemmas.

While the dilemmas are undoubtedly real, the letters – perhaps unconsciously – stick extremely close to the sub-genre of sexual fiction. They invariably trace sexual, emotional and marital issues and they always offer a narrative in certain distinctive ways. The form of the letters seems to be startlingly uniform; the language and details are invariably similar. I'm not trying to suggest that the letters are made up; just that the form is known and determines what is told and how it is told. It is hard to imagine a letter to a gardening magazine using the same language and criteria of significance: 'I'm twenty-two and today three leaves dropped off my rubber plant. I've had one rubber plant before which lived ten years. I threw it out when it got red spider. I'm very upset and anxious that I will lose a rubber plant again and this is making me depressed. Please tell me what to do.' Certain information is vital in problem-page stories which is not vital in other advice: age, previous (and current) sexual relations, how these affect your emotions, degree of openness with sexual partner, compatibility with the rest of society (parental approval, race and cultural background). Above all, the information has to be organized into a little story. Life is narrativized: this, then this, now what?

Problem pages then are a distinct genre of sexual fiction for writer and reader. They incite women to reveal and read about how an individual reached a certain point in her life, what the options are before her; they invite us to speculate on the causes and outcomes of sexual relations. The use of problem pages by women as readers and writers is part of the general way in which women are construed as those who investigate sexual relations, those who bear responsibility for sexual relations. Problem pages are the domestic end of sexual fiction, the chance an ordinary woman gets to confess in public and organize her thoughts and life crises as a novel (and therefore anticipate an ending). Irma Kurtz remarks, 'A writer will often say, "I feel so much better after writing to you. Thank you." And she will often request that a letter should not be printed. Writing is a catharsis, but to be effective the letter must be *sent* and not thrown in the rubbish bin' (*Guardian*, op. cit.).

The ideology behind this is clear. Speak out. It will make you feel better. Organize your crisis into a narrative, be honest and perhaps then you will see the causes, the reason why you feel like this. The letter is the first step to honesty and the practice of honesty, once learnt, will be easy to apply elsewhere. Take this confession further. The implication is that the letters published are not more significant for being published. They are only examples to the readers, examples of how much better it is to get it all off your chest, to learn to take the first painful steps towards discussing it with other people.

The injunction to reveal all about your sexual life, and to put all your scattered emotions into coherent speech, belongs to a general pattern given to sexuality in this society. Indeed, sexual relations generally are under a discursive injunction. These are the secrets that must be told. There has been an increase in the ways in which sexuality is talked about, medically, sociologically, statistically and legally. And with this increase in discussion there's also been an elevation of the significance of sexuality. Sexuality has been submitted to the demand that it should be analysed, explained and discussed. We are enjoined to confess our innermost feelings and thoughts about sexuality because they seem to be, in this society, the key to our personalities.

This pressure to confess all does not, however, affect the sexes eqůally. Women bear the burden of speech in this area. Women are incited to take responsibility for sexual relationships, to analyse, facilitate, interpret and ultimately to lubricate social and sexual relationships which have run into trouble. Perhaps this seems a paradoxical assertion. Elsewhere I might appear to be arguing that the sexual needs of men dominate cultural presentation of sexuality. Advertising and pornography appeal to men's fantasies of sexuality rather than women's, so much so that men's sexual needs sometimes appear as pressing, urgent, almost violent. This doesn't actually contradict my argument, for a split is created between what the sexes are assumed to have invested in the sexual structure. Men are assumed to have pressing *sexual* needs. Women have become the repository for the *emotional work* of the relationship. While men are incited to more and more complicated and novel forms of *sexual technique*, women are incited to shoulder the weight of *sexual consciousness*. Women are required to make sense of sexual relationships, they are meant to negotiate, explain, confess, keep the relationship in circulation. And when it fails, it falls to women to understand what happened or sort themselves out. Problem pages are the arena where this narrative of sexual consciousness is made public.

The exhortation to own up to your feelings and talk about sex is widespread, though it has reached a climax in popular sexology. Sex, once shrouded in modesty, is now wearing the loud checks of honesty. Talk through your feelings, share experiences and swap fantasies; 'We've got to let young people talk about sex, but we must make sure they understand what they are talking about. It's important they realize that sex isn't only about the act of intercourse, but about sharing experiences, establishing relationships' (Jane Cousins, *Woman's World*). The ultimate aim of sexology seems to be totally transparent emotions as regards sex. Past histories, revelations of mutual fantasies, disappointments, complexities, confessions: all of these, so we're told, aid the sexual sensations. Sex without these props is hardly worthy of the name.

But transparency doesn't just fall from the skies. Women are given the responsibility of making it work. If women own up, and talk freely, they will set an example for their men and make for a greater climate of emotional prosperity. In an article entitled 'Getting Your Man to Talk', *Cosmopolitan* (May 1980) tells women how to go about it: 'The right sort of *gentle* questioning about inner feelings can naturally help stimulate emotion, but be careful that you do not irritate your mate by probing too deeply. The best policy is to be as transparent as possible yourself. Then your partner is likely to respond by opening up in a way he has undoubtedly longed to do, perhaps for years.'

Being honest about yourself as women are in the problem pages will make you feel better. But it is only a beginning. There's a knock-on effect; others around you will acquire a taste for it. Everyone will soon be at it – confessing, admitting, sharing, and thereby enriching sexual life.

Women actually live out this command to speak and do the work of an emotional relationship. This much is clear from some of the sociological research on different speech patterns between men and women. Women do the domestic labour in routine social intercourse – 'How are you? Who are you? What do you do? Where do you live? Why the hell don't you ever say anything?' But women also do the equivalent shit work in the murky depths of sexual intercourse – 'What's upsetting you? Why don't you want to have sex? Is it something at work? Something I've said?' The role as facilitator of sticky social situations is shouldered even up to the bedroom.

Indeed, it is tempting to think that the whole sexual and social structure of our society might break down were it not for the heroic task which women perform in the cerebral regions. Conversations between men have long been recognized as resting at a relatively impersonal superficial level. Yet having at least one settled relationship with a woman is taken as a necessary sign of successful manhood, although men are not required to take up any responsibility for these relationships.

It is for this reason that I note problems with the injunction to sexual honesty which is currently directed towards women. This injunction takes no note of the social circumstances in which sexual relationships are still conducted. There are few pressures on men to change their way of being in the world, to change their inability to communicate, to start taking responsibility for the important things – children and other people. A tiny minority of men are directly touched by the desire to organize their emotional life differently. In general, material addressed to men – specialist magazines, TV programmes, pornography – confirms men in their traditional roles – powerful, detached from emotional life, and often exploitative in attitudes towards sex. In such a situation the pressure on women to talk makes women function as a currency between men. Women's speech sustains men's impersonal relationships between themselves.

There is a great deal that we need to explore within and about sexual relations. We need to understand why they often seem so disproportionately important and why they can become so obsessive; we need to understand why sexual relations have the capacity to hurt us so deeply; we need to understand why sexual relations awaken deep feelings of insecurity, rejection and possessiveness, or even call out destructive behaviour. We need to understand how sexual relations often follow patterns set by our primary experiences of dependency and how these patterns of dependency relate to external social structures. And these kinds of understanding will come only when we have learnt to talk through the defences and obssessional behaviour which obscure all this.

But as these discussions are currently directed, they merely endanger women further. They reproduce the belief that sexuality is the most important aspect of a woman's life, and encourage her to direct all her attention to an even greater labour in sexual relations. And, perhaps more dangerously, the discussions create the fiction that the only real structural problems between men and women are those which can be wished away by total transparency. In a society where men do have greater advantages than women, where men are brought up to disregard their emotions and often belittle women, no amount of speaking can guarantee that men will be able to respond in kind. Indeed there's surely an even greater risk that to be totally honest with someone who can't respond in kind might be even more hurtful.

Power resides not just in the fact of greater opportunity and dominance of social institutions; power is also lived out in emotional relationships. And men's economic, legal and political power has tended to be reflected in general masculine attitudes towards women, sexual relationships and child care. To 'own up' to someone, to be totally transparent about your needs and feelings, often means owning up to vulnerability, dependency and insecurities. Is it really safe that women, already structurally vulnerable, should yet further expose themselves? Is it really the case that men, illuminated by the bright light of their partners' transparency, will suddenly change their ways? Can conflict and distress, which may well be caused by the structural inequalities between men and women, really be solved within the interior of that relationship?

I can't help noticing that all this encouragement to women to speak, own up and confess doesn't include encouragement for women's talk to go beyond the confines of the bedroom walls. The pressure to speak is all directed inwards. Perhaps the speech will reach outsiders – the agony aunts, or some professional adviser. But it will soon be making its way back, back to the bedroom, back to the couple with all the misunderstandings and irrationality filtered out.

Our Song

Nowhere is sexual desire more obviously scripted and stage-managed than in the mishmash of music and chat directed at women during the day on popular radio. Sexual desire, attraction and love dominate not just as themes in the music but also make up a large part of the DJ's chatter. Forthcoming marriages, broken hearts, happy memories – these are the meat of radio discourse; relationships are at the heart of phone-ins; and radio dedications are from lover to lover. Popular music is broadcast into homes and workplaces during the day, presupposing a certain kind of predominantly female audience. The packaging of the music engages the emotions of this female audience, focusing attention on sexual relationships and in particular requiring the listener to think about her own sexual and emotional involvements.

Radio dedications are very explicitly associated with emotional involvements. Listeners are encouraged to dedicate records to their loved ones. And, in spite of pressure on radio only to play a small and limited number of records in the current charts, there are slots where listeners can request particular records connected with particular memories. London's commercial radio station, Capital, has a variety of slots during the day where these personal memories can be recounted. Radio One also has a morning programme where listeners reveal startlingly personal associations.

Capital Radio sometimes has a 'top six' slot where listeners, who are almost invariably female, are invited to present their favourite six records. These records are usually framed by the DJ's questions: 'Why is this record so significant for you?'; 'Is there any special reason for this record?' And if the woman starts with an explanation of why she likes the music of the Rolling Stones, she's brought quickly back in line, 'Does it have happy memories for you?'

When the women play the game, they answer with memories of first boyfriends, disco-dancing, courting future husbands, pleasurable associations such as 'the first time I kissed my husband'. Integrating popular music with these kinds of memories, usually from women now working at home with young children, represents an interesting manoeuvre. Like the linking of current 'hits' to dedications between lovers and spouses, it represents the use of popular music to give certain meanings to the lives of women listening to the radio during the day.

A habitual connection is made between popular music and the

personal memories of women. It links the use of music at discos,
parties and generally in young people's lives to the relatively settled
domestic settings of the radio audience. Perhaps though there's a
contradiction between the way music is used at parties and the way
radio offers it up to women.

Popular music has its greatest impact as concerts for the serious
followers and as dancing music at discos and parties. At one level,
contemporary music works as a means of subgroup identification.
Styles of dress operate as signals about what kind of music is liked.
Because of this a whole series of other preferences can be read off –
political, class and sexual orientations. But music is also more
generally significant. It is music which provides the background to
the social exchanges which take place at parties and discos.

Parties and discos are the places where explicit expression of
sexual feelings is sanctioned. Attraction can be felt, desire expressed,
obsessions tolerated. Parties are the modern carnivals: the chance to
transgress the normal rules of personal behaviour. They are not just
opportunities to talk to people and to enjoy dancing. They are above
all meant to be significantly different from everyday social intercourse – events to be dressed for, events where you can expect to do
'excessive' things like drinking too much, yet be forgiven. Parties
often don't start till after pub closing time, all part of the need to
establish their transgressive identity. People hang around till the
small hours, waiting to time their appearance just right. The party
has to be in full swing; it has to be safely established as a different
event, where the everyday routine intercourse and strictures on
behaviour can be suspended.

In *Jackie*, a magazine for teenage girls, the party or disco features
as this symbolic place where sexual encounters are staged and
enacted. There are endless preparations for the party, endless
anxieties about what might and might not happen. And the party is
where decisive events occur. There's the joy of being noticed by the
'fancied bloke' and the heartbreak of the boyfriend being 'pinched'
by the best friend. The party establishes who's going with whom,
which people can't keep their eyes off each other, and who is
obsessed with whom.

At parties, it is the rhythm and beat of the music that matters.
These elements are crucial to the popularity of certain groups or
records for dancing. They give the necessary background to a highly
ritualized style of visual display. Rhythms of popular music are
geared towards a kind of dancing where the body is more often

displayed than touched. Disco-dancing, in spite of its insistent ambience of sexuality, still does not provide more intimate physical contact than more formal styles of dancing. Just like the forms of intercourse at parties, dancing is all about innuendo, all about hinting at sex rather than just doing it out there in the centre of the room.

Briefly, then, parties are rich events, full of innuendo, places where ambiguous but heightened exchanges can take place – food for thought, pleasure or grief afterwards. Parties are excessive social exchanges. Highly ritualized they may be, but they are also moments in the construction of an ambience of attraction, desire, fruition, disappointment. These are the moments where the most intimate emotions can be negotiated most publicly, exaggerated in pleasure precisely because of the to and fro between intimate knowledge and public display.

But when we come to the use of popular music on daytime radio, we find the ambiguity, the excessive nature of parties harnessed to the personal associations of settled individuals. Here, the strength and wildness of desire is controlled, sanitized. Listening to music on the radio foregrounds the lyrics. The radio is where people often become familiar with the lyrics of current songs. It is how the words pass unmediated into our unconsciousness, returning to take us by surprise when we find ourselves singing along to words we didn't realize we knew.

And listening to the lyrics we find some intriguing factors. In spite of the growth in political music or music where the lyrics raise social issues, popular music is still absolutely dominated by reference to sexual attraction, sexual encounter, and the detailing of a love affair. To listen carefully to the words of a record can be a curious experience; it is like eavesdropping on an intimate conversation or argument between lovers, or like getting a crossed line on the telephone and listening, embarrassed and fascinated, to personal revelations: The lyrics detail the burning desire which a lover's kiss can induce, or stormy nights of unbroken sleep. They describe sweet dreams of a departed lover, sweet dreams instead of hate and anger. Many current songs are like fragments of a narrative, a sudden exposure of a moment in a relationship. Don't leave me, the lyrics plead, my life will fall apart, you'll destroy me, break my heart. Or we hear the other side: it's painful, I know, but I have to go. We've hurt each other enough, I have to leave.

Most striking about these lyrics is their insistent mode of communication. It is an exchange from one individual to another: my love for you can't be stopped; I'm burning with my desire: or, can you really want to hurt me, can you really want to leave? The songs detail a particular emotional state and address it to *you* as if you were the person in question, only you. This is the way the records take on an intensely personal meaning. Not only do the rhythms and beat participate in an atmosphere redolent with the budding or breaking of a relationship, but the lyrics go over again and again a limited number of sexual experiences: attraction, satisfaction, heartbreak, jealousy, new relationship.

In some respects, these lyrics are very odd, because until quite recently the pop industry has been dominated by men. Yet the lyrics reveal men time and time again speaking and singing and indeed thinking in ways that contradict how men present themselves outside the lyrics of pop songs. Here are men helplessly passionate, endlessly vulnerable, constant in love even in the face of insuperable odds. Here are men inconsolable and heartbroken, and men sensitive and gentle in their seductions – strange when we ponder on how often women bemoan men's often callous attitude to sex, men's insensitivity within relationships, and men's lack of constancy in love.

Could it be that these lyrics correspond to a fantasy that women have, that men really talk and think like women? Or is the crooning, passionate gentleness of men in these records an expression of tenderness which normal social intercourse prohibits? Is it that, in pop records, all the repressed speech and thought about relationships come tumbling out, aimed at seduction?

Whatever the explanation, one thing is sure. The chatter of DJs on radio stations uses this dialogue to very specific ends. The broken affairs of the listeners, their divorces, their jealousy, their new relationships are all given meaning by this kind of record. And the DJs talk in a way which reinforces the sense that all this – the records, the lyrics, and his chatter – are addressed just to you as an individual. It is as if somehow, the DJ knows all about you and is talking just to you: 'Here's Claire Rayner to answer your problems' ... 'If you're a Sagittarian ...' ... 'Do you want to win a free lunch?' The address is never to a collectivity but always to an individual. It reinforces the sense created by the records. It is *your* life being talked about, the emotions generated by the records are for *you*, the problems to be addressed will be *yours*.

The more direct the link has become with the individual listener, through the medium of phone-ins or contests, the more intimate and important this sense of the individual has become. Direct feedback introduces the possibility of realizing just what a diversity of people and lives makes up our society, how differently middle-class people live, and what a difference it makes to be a member of an ethnic minority in a racist society. But if all the chatter and the direct links with the listeners can find a common denominator, the radio can address a mass audience while appearing only to talk intimately to an individual. And sexual desire has been constructed as the daytime lowest common denominator. Reduced to a superficial description – attraction, making love, commitment and abandonment – it could be said to happen to all of us all the time. Of course, if you care to go past the superficial description, *what* happens and *how it happens* and *why* it happens differ radically from one individual to another. Class and race make a difference to start with, but there are also differences in how we experience sexual relationships and what meaning they have in relation to the rest of our lives and friendship. There are differences in what sex means to different people; they often handle things like rejection quite differently. All of these variants depend on personal, social and cultural backgrounds.

But popular radio works in a definite way to limit the meanings of these emotions. They are kept at a superficial level of description and they are assumed to be within certain universal forms. They are assumed to be heterosexual and exclusive. Marriage and monogamy appear as the inevitable outcome of 'meeting a man' and 'dating'. Sexual attraction is left as something mysterious. It just happens. Sometimes it is mutual, sometimes it is not. If it is not, we all know how bad that is; if things go wrong, we are consoled 'it just didn't work out'. A broken relationship is like death, gone for ever. No cause, no explanation, no reprieve. And it is no coincidence that the mourning of the songs is used also for memories of death. Everything is just part of life's rich pattern; there's no explanation and it's the same for everyone. Radio chatter constructs this base line of sexual desire and uses it to bond the listener into a particular form of address. The listener is lured by a promise; you are special (the individual addressed) but your life and experiences are exactly the same as everyone else's.

The only difference permitted by radio discourse is between age groups, which are seen merely as different points on the same kind of life continuity. There's no sense that the audience might be divided on political, economic or racial grounds; no sense created that sexual desire might not be heterosexual or predictable, that sexual desire might in fact be anarchic and transgressive as it often is at parties. Daytime radio works to validate the choices which women have made. The phase of their lives when they went to parties, experienced their carnival of emotions, is treated nostalgically as part of a comfortable personal history. Daytime radio tells women who are isolated and at home, and possibly very fed up, that the choices which they made were OK. Everyone makes these choices all the time. And sexual relations, women are told, are after all the most important, most universal aspect of our selves. Sexual relations are presented in such a way as to suggest a national interest, a collectivity with identical interests and identical experiences. Here is a crucial way in which women's desire, controlled and sanitized, is stage-managed to suppress differences between groups and conflicts of interest in a divided nation.[1]

[1] For further reading on the subject of women and radio, see the Women's Airwaves section of 'Local Radio in London' by the Local Radio Workshop; Anne Karpf's 'Women and Radio' in *Women's Studies International Quarterly* 1980, vol. 3; and Moss and Higgins, *Sounds Real*, University of Queensland, 1982.

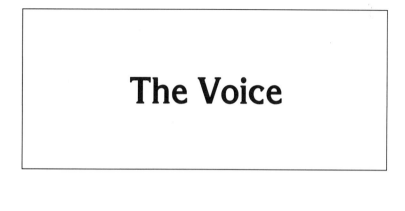

The Voice

Language is meant to be about communication. People use language to explain themselves, to exchange ideas and feelings with other individuals. Language reaches out across the gulf between two individuals and joins them together in the act of communication. And a shared use of a national language is supposed to reflect a shared sense of social identity. We can all speak to each other. OK, misunderstandings quite obviously arise; language doesn't always do its job. But in commonsense concepts of language, there's a naïve optimism: the more you talk, the more you are likely to understand. If we keep on talking, we'll be able to find out what each other really thinks.

In fact, language does as much to keep us apart as it helps us to understand and share. Because language doesn't exist in any abstract way; language only exists as distinct ways of talking, as different voices used by groups in specific contexts. And some of the distinctive forms of speech in circulation in our society do as much to stop people communicating with one another as they do to aid communication. Some recognizable modes of talking, and recognizable vocabularies, hide connections between events and obscure differences between people.

As a society we certainly hear far more voices than our predecessors. Because of the so-called 'mass' media, we are exposed to a far greater weight of speech. There are voices issuing out of the radio and the television; there's written matter uninvited through the door, and pages of speech offered in newspapers and magazines. There's no need to be in silence. Teachers have frequently noted that children of today have been exposed to far more speech than in previous periods, where, before school, the child might only have heard parents, parents' friends or their siblings. Just at the level of vocabulary, children now have a far wider range. It should follow that with this great explosion of voices, we should have more and more refined speech, a language of greater precision and subtlety, a higher ability to explain and understand connections, and understand what other people are trying to say.

Actually the sheer volume of speech makes little difference to the possibility of understanding, because language doesn't work in this way. Speech comes to us ordered by distinct ways of talking, using distinct modes of address; it is used to make some connections and exclude others. Take the way in which the IRN reported on the

Conservative Party's anti-CND advertising campaign. On 13 February 1983 the IRN reported that 'CND's outburst followed the Prime Minister's speech yesterday'. It is quite obvious what's happening here: CND has 'outbursts' and the Prime Minister makes 'speeches'. This is using language to set up significant oppositions: outburst/speech; wild/orderly; irrational/rational. This way of talking obviates the need for the statement, 'This news agency agrees with the Prime Minister and opposes the tactics of CND.' The language does the work; it creates an impression of tactics – rational ones versus irrational ones – where any sensible person would know which was right. In short, the kind of language used, the oppositions it sets up, the connections and associations it provokes, determine what can be thought. It doesn't make that much difference if there's an impressive bulk of communication when what gets communicated limits what can be thought.

It is not just that language is ordered into discursive unities which coerce the listener into sharing the assumptions of the group using this language. The *form* of address currently in dominance within the 'mass' media also works to limit communication, to keep people apart. Take advertisements, TV, and radio. To use the term 'mass' media is really to mislead. Because although these forms of communication aim at (and succeed, it seems) in reaching audiences of millions, they do not presuppose a mass audience. All the speech is directed towards *an individual*.

Nowhere is this clearer than in the case of advertising. Take the experience of travelling by train, or travelling by underground in London. As often as not people travel alone. Yet there are so many other people around, the experience could hardly be described as solitary. Indeed such an experience brings the individual very closely into contact with strangers. It is clear from anthropological studies that the encounter with strangers usually requires some recognized social ritual to lessen anxiety about the possible hostility of a strange individual. Claude Lévi-Strauss described this as the need to neutralize the problem of otherness, to establish a sense of reciprocity, of belonging to the same community.[1]

To give an example of this, Lévi-Strauss described a routine scene in a French restaurant. Two individuals sit close to each other but at different tables; each has a carafe of wine on the table. Although the wine in the carafes is identical, it is polite for each to pour the other a

[1] See C. Lévi-Strauss, *The Elementary Structures of Kinship*, Eyre and Spottiswoode, 1949.

glass of wine from his/her carafe. After that they can ignore each other with good conscience.

The anthropologist saw behind this traditional politeness a ritual of exchange, a mutual recognition of the other person as separate and different, potentially hostile until some exchange establishes communication. British society is almost completely bankrupt in such rituals; even handshaking is now largely disregarded. There are precious few rituals by which we can establish our connection with new people. Travelling with a crowd the anxiety can become acute; there are moments of unearthly stillness if the train stops unexpectedly. Everyone wants the silence broken, no one wants to be heard. It requires a 'joker' to cut through the potential hysteria, someone who allows the crowd to experience collective solidarity in amusement.

Yet in this uneasy exposure to strangers, and in this uncanny and crowded silence, we are constantly engaged in communication. 'Something's Alpened to your Porridge,' we are told; 'You can tell at a glance' we are reminded; 'Your money will be safe with us.' Someone out there on the walls is talking to us after all. Even when the ads don't address us specifically as individuals, they nevertheless chatter at us, giving us good advice: 'Smash an Egg today.' Selling nothing but a blank space for other advertisements, the voice is still insistent: 'Makes Passers Buy'. And by the time we're on the mechanical stairways slogging home, it's getting pretty cheeky, 'Watch sales escalate.'

Our attention is most thoroughly engaged by the use of puns and tricks of language. Advertisements for tights and stockings mine a rich seam of puns to accompany their visual speciality – disembodied limbs: 'Beats the pants off trousers' and 'They're an asset when it's frozen'. No slacking allowed; the reader really has to do some work sorting out these meanings. Advanced advertisement readers even get engaged in in-jokes, references to previous advertising campaigns; 'Guinnless isn't Good for You', and, 'Polo. The mint with the less fattening centre'. Rawlings, a tonic water company, advertised its product directly by reference to the 'Sssh, you know who' campaign of its rivals: 'We knew how before Sssh, you know who.' If you go about your business on the streets, if you travel on public transport, open a magazine or paper, a thousand voices clamour for attention.

Isolated in a crowd, there's an incessant call to attention: 'Hey, you. Read this. It may make you laugh!' The mind is constantly drawn into a game, a game of decipherment. There is a constant dialogue, but with a multitude of messages rather than with another person. And the messages have but a single voice. Humorous, witty, direct. They could be the same person speaking at us, including us in the meanings, inviting us to understand, and encouraging us to consume. Walls don't have ears any more but they do have voices.

Everyone in this society suffers from imaginary conversations with the walls. But women seem to be the privileged recipients of this verbal seduction. On the radio and in magazines, for instance, women are encouraged to *respond*, to engage in dialogue with this personal address of the impersonal media. Women's direct speech is often required. Women are encouraged to phone or write in. Women are encouraged to tell all. And women are interrogated, subjected to quizzes and the surveys which women's magazines so love to run. Is it because women can be more isolated than men that there's more susceptibility to communication, even if it is with institutions?

Perhaps this is why the speech directed at women has an almost urgent tone of intimacy wooing them into dialogue with institutions. In a TV interview, Iris Burton, editor of *Woman's Own*, spoke with pride of how her readership would write to her as if they knew her personally.[2] And that's nice, she said, it reflects how the readers are feeling about the magazine. Readers clearly are required to think about magazines as their friends.

Actually the kinds of writing characteristic of women's magazines work within definite conventions which aim at eliciting this personal and immediate response. The articles in women's magazines regularly adopt this pseudo-personal tone, establishing a sense of the writers as real individuals and readers as receivers of intimate knowledge. I call it pseudo-personal because only certain information is forthcoming, and only some kinds of writing encouraged. Anecdotal or opinionated, the discourse is peppered with little anecdotes: 'The lower fifth used to tuck their fags in their navy blues, and sneak off for a smoke behind the garden shed,' or 'My first husband never used to change his pants.' Then there will follow an article about education or divorce. We are allowed intimate revelations about where the journalist lives, her class background, school outings, or the odd anecdote about married life. One or two personal memories, and then on to a more impersonal, factual mode. The assumption is that the reader will relate only to a serious well-

[2] On 'Inside Women's Magazines', Director M. Allinson, Research, M. Cunliffe, BBC, 1983.

researched article through wity, personal memories, especially if the journalist reveals herself to be human and fallible.

This is also true of the presentation of opinions. Opinions are OK if they are motivated by personal experience, but not so readily acceptable if they stem from political or theoretical commitments.

These forms of writing could probably be justified on the best possible grounds – they present important issues to women in an accessible way. But they also represent a way of talking which excludes as much as it offers, for very great assumptions are made about who an 'ordinary' woman is, what she wants to read and what she thinks. In offering an intensely personal address and assuming a personal involvement, the article can claim to represent the ordinary woman who after all is pretty reasonable and doesn't like any 'extremism'. In the *Woman* column (21 August 1982) 'You and Us', the editor, Jane Reed, told us what 'We think'; 'The hard-liner feminists have made us feel guilty for enjoying dressing up, putting on make-up, looking after families, doing housework, . . . now they're after the pleasurable side of cooking.' I was amused on reading this suddenly to realize that 'us' and 'we' did not after all include me since it was my views on food pornography which were being attacked!

It is strange to realize that women are at the heart of this discursive seduction; the response that the public voices constantly seek is women's. It is even stranger when we consider how much women are in fact silenced in personal exchanges. There has been plenty of research conducted in the field of socio-linguistics on what happens when men and women speak to each other, and the evidence suggests that in a mixed group, women speak far less than men. And, when women do speak, they often use language in a way which supports men's verbal dominance. Women are encouraged to laugh at men's jokes, and to ask questions which encourage men to speak. Men, it seems, do not return the compliment. Less well charted and more nebulous is the way in which *what* women say is also marginalized by men. When women speak in public, men frequently dismiss women's contributions as off the point or not worth taking seriously. Yet this is only because men have evolved a particular way of talking with each other, and often a set of priorities which women probably don't share. Men take up more space than women with their speech, filling the air with their way of talking, their jokes, their sense of priorities, and frequently belittling women who attempt to talk. I have been witness to a woman called a 'harpy' for disagreeing with a male colleague, and to women dismissed as 'shrill' when they challenged the priorities set by men.

Women are incited to communicate with the direct address of media institutions but marginalized in real speech between men and women. The discursive bombardment does not enlarge what can be said or thought; it offers only limited ways of seeing and thinking about the world. No wonder women's speech sometimes sounds dominated by discontent. Our attention is required but our speech is not heard. We must understand the messages of others, but we cannot expect to be understood ourselves.

PART IV

THE
STORY

The Royals

'The Royals' is the longest-running soap opera in Britain. One branch of the media can always be relied on to carry the next instalment – one or other of the daily newspapers, a television news report, or a women's magazine, invariably has something on the latest developments in the Royal family. We have become just as intimate with the doings of the folk from Buckingham Palace as we have with the folk from Southfork Ranch. The romances, weddings, births and deaths, the conflicts and rivalries, are all made available to us. And like any good soap opera, 'The Royals' has its ardent fans and its bitter opponents.

In the 1950s, the television soap opera found its feet. Using the fact of the permanent domestic presence of the television, a form of narrative developed which could, like life, go on almost indefinitely.[1]

Each episode was to be a microcosm of drama and intrigue. And in that very period, the press began to treat 'The Royals' differently. Playing down 'statesmanship' and aristocracy, the public were treated to more and more intimate revelations and points of speculation about the young family of Queen Elizabeth. Is it just coincidence that in this postwar period, when anachronistic institutions might have been cleared away, the press produced a new-style monarchy – familial, more accessible and almost ordinary? Or was it that an infallible format had been discovered? Was it that 'The Royals', like a soap opera, offered a rich vein of intimate revelations, based 'roughly on reality', which never has to end, which never has to be the subject of political debate? Who, after all, is going to call for the abdication of Miss Ellie?

Royal soap is based on the same narrative structures as 'Dallas'. It offers all the pleasures of a good family melodrama. Like 'Dallas', it is the long-running story of an extremely wealthy and powerful family. The two soap operas share the same preoccupations: the unity of the family; family wealth; dynastic considerations like inheritance and fertility; sexual promiscuity; family duty; and alliances with outsiders/rivals/lower orders. The fact that 'The Royals' is loosely based on reality only adds to its fascination. Statements from the Royal press office attempt to check gross distortions; but this voice of truth only adds to the pleasurable activity of comparing reports, and building up a hierarchy of reliable

[1] For an account of TV narratives, see J. Ellis, *Visible Fictions*, Routledge and Kegan Paul, 1982.

sources. All our knowledge of the Royals is more or less fictional, based on media stories and the occasional sighting. We have no more direct knowledge of the Royals than of any other fictional TV character, and seeing the Queen in the flesh isn't that different from seeing the actress who plays Miss Ellie.

It doesn't matter that there's a real-life family behind the story. What matters is the *way* the story is told; some elements are treated as highly significant, others are not even dealt with. And the Royal family is presented exactly according to the conventions of a family melodrama. 'The Royals' doesn't just follow life as it is, because 'life as it is' is presented differently by different narrative genres. Narrative is, in general, the lineal organization of events across time, and events are helped along by the functions or acts of various protagonists in the story. There are, however, wide divergences between genres as to what events are significant, how important the characters are in relation to the action, and so on. In a thriller, for instance, the narrative starts with a disruption and an enigma. The rest of the narrative will then be geared to unravelling these events and restoring the state of order which existed before the book began. Depending on the particular sub-genre of thriller, the characters will be more or less significant. Some writers emphasize the psychological motivation of characters; others use the characters merely as springboards for a chase sequence or an obligatory sex scene. Even stories which deal with more 'ordinary' concerns organize their elements differently. Westerns, for example, concentrate on work in the family homestead; threats to the family from sexual infidelity; or attacks by outsiders (the Indians). The preoccupations are work, courage, strength, and initiative. The birth of a baby, a wedding, or the family background of the characters are not the most significant events.

A family melodrama is preoccupied with sexual relations, marriage, the unity of the family, internal conflict within the family, and the disintegration of the family which is usually embodied in the threat of 'outsiders' or 'the problem of the modern woman'. The story stays as close as possible to the everyday. It doesn't include enigmas and supernatural happenings, as did the American parody of soap operas, 'Soap', when one of the 'characters' was beamed into a spaceship in the middle of a domestic conflict. And family melodramas do not deal with politics, workplace conflicts or social issues, except as they affect the family.

Some family melodramas have as their central aim the elevation of the particular family as representative of all human (or national) emotions. 'The Royals' have this position, just like the Ewings. The Ewings are elevated by extreme wealth; the Royals by extreme nobility. The function of this elevated status is the same for both though: it enables us to ask how are family conflicts and choices lived out in the family that has everything? The Archbishop of Canterbury gave an address at the wedding between Prince Charles and Lady Diana which made this archetypal function quite clear. The wedding, he said, may look like a fairy tale, but it is only the same step that everybody has to take; 'At the centre of a nation's life, there is a bewildering kaleidoscope of events, peopled by a huge and ever-changing cast of politicians and personalities. We are fortunate in having at the heart of our national life another ingredient, the presence of a family, providing a sense of continuity and *pointing to the most profound themes of human life* which do not change from century to century' (Official Programme for the Royal Wedding, my emphasis).

The Ewings and the Royals may have an elevated status but their problems and conflicts are meant to be those which all families share. These conflicts and problems are expressed through a series of oppositions in the narrative. It is the function of the characters to carry one or other of the terms in the opposition. The oppositions in this kind of family melodrama revolve around: rebel/conformist; promiscuous/faithful; good mother/bad mother; good son or daughter/bad son or daughter; nobility/commoner; rightful (biological) heir/rival claim.

'Dallas' is able to offer fairly fixed functions for its characters. Thus JR can remain consistently rotten. In this authentic fiction, it is possible to have one really nasty character. After all, in the cut-throat world of big business, this is relatively plausible, perhaps even acceptable. The Royals, however, could not afford the luxury of a consistent rotter. Because their fictional status is more ambiguous it would be dangerous to have one truly scheming member. Such a person in a world of extraordinary privilege, which is nevertheless granted by the goodwill of the people, would be far too problematic. The question might well be asked: why should we tolerate these people? Instead the oppositions between good and evil, deserving and undeserving, are distributed among a number of characters. The function of villainy, in short, is distributed among a number of characters who can then carry a single attribute of 'rottenness' – promiscuity, coldness, drunkenness. But no character in 'The Royals' is allowed to have all these characteristics at one time.

In fact the way in which the narrative functions are split up among the different Royal characters gives us a good idea about the structures and emotions to which the Royal appeal is addressed. Take the marriage of Prince Charles to Lady Diana. Lady Diana introduced a new element to the story of 'The Royals'; with her arrival several characters had to take a step sideways or change their narrative function. Princess Anne, from being basically a good sport, was promptly given the status of 'ugly sister'. Papers carried reports of her bitchy remarks about Lady Di and rumours were in circulation about the disintegration of her marriage. Mark Phillips, it was alleged, had gone off with a lady newsreader; hardly surprising, the papers continued, because Princess Anne was such a *bad* mother. The sudden indulgence of hostility towards Princess Anne (a hostility which has always been lurking beneath the surface) could suddenly appear because the Royals now had a truly charming, innocent, but sexually attractive Princess. Princess Anne was then transferred to the other side of the classic oppositions accruing to aristocratic women. Lady Di carried the gracious, gentle attributes; Princess Anne, on the other hand was arrogant, bitchy, ungainly. Clearly it became much safer to give Princess Anne these qualities once her children were displaced from the Royal succession.

Prior to the introduction of Princess Diana, the function of the undeserving Royal woman was fulfilled by Princess Margaret. The major opposition of good and bad was played out around the sisters, Elizabeth and Margaret. Margaret, at first a tragically thwarted lover, settled into her press position as a semi-alcoholic, difficult, divorced woman over whose sexual morality, it was alleged, hung a very large question mark. The Queen on the other hand was shy, dutiful, a good mother and a tactful woman – her only faults were the occasional signs of bad dress sense. So 'wicked' did Margaret become that even her commoner husband, the photographer Snowdon, was elevated to the position of patient, hard-working, long-suffering husband. Margaret for a long time has carried the connotations of the decadent and undeserving side of wealth. The splitting of the functions between characters is very apparent in the way her extended holidays in Mustique have been treated. These holidays are not worth so much as a mention when the other Royals go, but in Margaret's case they instantly symbolize the decadent and undeserving, the indulgent and weak side of wealth. Since the Charles and Di wedding, however, Margaret has been rehabilitated somewhat; we now see articles on how she has taken herself in hand, sorted out her life. This rehabilitation can probably last only while one of the other characters is carrying some of the attributes of decadence.

Margaret has also been a crucial figure in the speculation about whether royalty will make an alliance with an 'outsider'. And since her divorce from Lord Snowdon, she has been restored as a character able to bear speculation about what kind of sexual alliance royalty will make. Prior to his marriage to Lady Di, Prince Charles was the most important point of speculation on this subject. The Royal Wedding in fact produced a drastic change in the structural function of Charles. From Royal romancer travelling through the debutante set, he now takes up the position of Bobby Ewing, the faithful and devoted husband to the child bride. And once safely established as devoted husband and father, it was only a matter of time before questions were asked about whether he was also long-suffering, put upon by a wilful woman more concerned with getting her figure back than with her duties as a Royal mother: 'So shy Di became, first, the diet-obsessed anorexic Di, then hen-pecking, scolding Di, and now the little madam or fiend, or spoilt brat according to whom you read' (*Sunday Times*, 23 January 1983).

It is no coincidence that, as Charles is put through the possible options for good husband, another Royal romancer is brought to the centre of the stage. Known as 'Randy Andy', Prince Andrew was promptly cast as 'The Royals'' new Casanova. The Casanova function also becomes clear in his hands: will the Royals ever be tempted outside their ranks? Interestingly, Randy Andy obliges with another requirement which Prince Charles never properly fulfilled. Andrew, they say, does it with models and small-time pornography artistes whereas Charles remained largely within the aristocracy even if some of them were 'bad girls': 'The Royal dating game has never been easy. Not for any of the Queen's children. But, for Prince Andrew, with his chocolate box good looks, flashing smile and penchant for models and beauty queens, it has been the most complex of rituals' (*Daily Express*, 1 November 1982). The sexual alliances of these Princes have in essence hinged on the question of whether or not they will 'fall in love' with an outsider. All through Charles's hunt for an acceptable bride, there was speculation about whether love would get him into trouble – a Catholic, a divorcee, a commoner – we were all dying for it to happen. The narrative was just crying out for a trial in the name of love. Would he fall for someone and have to sacrifice everything, as the Duke of Windsor

did before him? It is interesting to remember in passing that the Duke
of Windsor's story readily adapted itself to an up-market soap opera.

This, of course, is a crucial element in a good family melodrama.
A tension is required between the requirements of family duty and
the wayward nature of love (so the ideology runs) which could strike
any time and endanger the unity or survival of the family. In
'Dallas', this narrative function is carried by Bobby. Like Romeo
and Juliet, the Ewings have a rival family but, being what it is, love
is no respecter of other people's prejudice. Bobby Ewing 'falls in
love' with Pamela Barnes, the daughter of the rival family.
Henceforth the narrative has a gratifying tension between family
duty and love of someone who threatens that unity.

With Lady Di the media found a way of compromising the public
desire for a love match with the actual constraints on Charles to
marry an aristocratic virgin. Lady Di, with impeccable sexual and
class credentials, was also sufficiently young and waif-like to satisfy
the desire for a marriage to an outsider, or the girl next door.
Deserted by her mother, in the shadow of her elder sister, sheltered
and shy, Lady Di didn't have the overt appearance of a highly
appropriate and eligible match. She could be seen as young,
innocent and beautiful, loved for what she was rather than for her
suitability.

In stories of family dramas and intrigues, there usually has to be
one figure who represents stability, whose good qualities validate all
the other comings and goings. In 'Dallas' there's Miss Ellie; in 'The
Royals', the Queen Mother. These figures are the female heads of
family. Now powerless, they are above the ambitions, promiscuity,
and intrigue of the junior members. These characters have been in
power at one time – they understand power – but they are now
above it. The best and most worthy aspects of the family are
invested in these figures. Gentle, kindly, understanding and
humane, these are the characters who, in the end, validate the whole
story.

These are the structural functions of the characters, but they don't
fully explain why these family melodramas have such appeal. That
appeal undoubtedly comes from the very successful combination of
the 'cosmic' (Christian) themes of good and evil, deserving and
undeserving, love and duty, and a very ordinary series of preoccupations. Even if the options facing these ideal families are somewhat
rarefied, the family is presented as just an ordinary family confronting the options of modern life.

It is easier to see how melodrama is influenced by certain social developments if it is a form of melodrama belonging to a past period. So, it is easy now to look at film melodramas of the 1950s and see a whole series of preoccupations about women's sexuality. The fifties films dealt with the effect of women's autonomous sexuality on the family; the themes are adultery, sexual choices, split loyalties. The preoccupations haunting contemporary family melodramas are no longer the dire consequences of female sexuality. Family melodramas are now obsessed with the question of what options there are for the family, and this question is particularly centred on 'the problem of the modern woman'. The themes of contemporary melodramas are sexual promiscuity, divorce, remarriage, styles of parenthood, the working woman. Just as millions followed the struggle over the custody of JR's child, so millions followed with fascination the accounts of Lady Di's upbringing by her divorced father. The Wedding itself was a focus for speculation on changed attitudes to family ruptures: 'Diana will of course be given away by her father, although a few years ago this could have been a problem because he and her mother are divorced. In the past there may have been some hesitation in inviting her parents *and* their new partners. However, a precedent was set in 1960 – Lord Snowdon's parents were also divorced and even though Ronald Armstrong-Jones had married a third time, both he and his wife were at the ceremony' (*Woman's Own* Engagement Special).

Another series of options relate to the question of how the Royals will bring up their children. Will Lady Di have a Leboyer birth? Will she breast-feed? Will she be a formal or informal mother: 'Sharing and warmth will be the basis of Diana's style of motherhood. This child will benefit from the most tactile contact with his mother of any of the royal babies so far' (The Free Giant Royal Baby Poster, *Woman's Own*, 4 September 1982). Then there's the question of what role Prince Charles will play. Will he be a modern father and participate in caring for the child? Charles carrying his 'eight-week-old son' is sufficient subject-matter for a photo captioned 'Holding the Baby'. There's also the question of whether Diana should be with the child as much as possible or leave him while she carries out her public duties: 'Prince William may fly to Australia with his parents next spring ... one of Britain's top paediatricians said: "I'm not talking specifically about the young prince, but as a generalization it's ideal for a child to be kept with his mother for the whole of the first year as much as possible."'

(Daily Express, 1 November 1982). However remote the lives of the inhabitants of Buckingham Palace, their fictionalized lives are constructed around a number of dilemmas which are just as significant for people of entirely different social and economic groups.

In our very different ways, without the privileges and without the constraints of traditions, women are confronted constantly with family issues – marriage or not marriage, children or not children, divorce, custody, how to bring up children. These aren't trivial and unimportant issues. Women's opportunities and indeed often our happiness rest on how we resolve these questions. But having said that 'The Royals' addresses choices faced by all women, it is also quite true that it does so from a peculiarly 'traditionalist' stand-point. In the world of 'The Royals', there aren't really any options outside the family, nor is there any issue of female independence and autonomy. All the 'problems' faced by the modern woman are reduced to choices within the family. Divorce becomes merely a matter of how to be tactful at the next wedding, birth is reduced to an issue of breast-feeding or not rather than an event which might involve loss of autonomy. Even 'Dallas' is slightly more open than 'The Royals' to discourses on female independence. For the Royals there's not a moment's hesitation in producing Lady Di as a modern heroine even though she married at twenty, was a mother by twenty-one, and had never had any sexual experience outside marriage.

Not only does 'The Royals' accomplish a repression of questions of female independence, it also accomplishes a repression of political and economic factors. The 'outside' of the Royal family is not working women and men who have little economic power and little control over their own lives. The 'outside' of royalty is aristocratic business men and show-biz. It is within this grouping that the Royals might make an alliance, as seen in the flirtations of Margaret and Randy Andy. The 'outside' of the Royals is the fashion world, the glamorous world of actresses, models, pop stars, and nightclub entertainers. These people are represented as somehow 'ordinary' in spite of the fact that they, like the Royals, represent an over-privileged, under-talented group. The 'outside' only ever intrudes into the unity of the family through sexual alliance; it is through love that the Royals are to brought into contact with people of a lesser order, not through conflict between groups who have different economic and social realities. The centrality given to the sexual alliance obscures the other kind of relations which the Crown might have, relations of landlords and tenants, relations between those with power and privilege and those with nothing.

The centrality which sexual alliance has in the family melodrama isn't just a wilful plot thought up by 'The Royals'. It reflects a prevalent belief that people, especially women, can advance their social position through sexual alliance. Being a beautiful actress or top model is seen as a route to power; powerful men will be attracted by star qualities. Indeed this belief is one of the important ways in which real differences in material circumstances are obscured. Women can make it on the basis of their beauty. Again this theme is widespread; it is common in romantic fiction where girls with ordinary backgrounds and extraordinary beauty attract wealthy men.

'The Royals' as a family melodrama works over choices that are real for many women and does it in such a way as to guarantee narrative interest. But the problem is that the Royal family isn't only a fiction. It is sustained as a fiction when it also represents political and economic privileges, and political and economic preferences. The way in which the story is told means that we never have to deal with the Royal family as a political institution; we only have to think about human behaviour, human emotions, and choices restricted to the family. 'The Royals' eternalizes traditional values, glorifies women's route to power through individual sexual attraction, and defines women as exclusively bound up with these values.

The True Story of How I Became My Own Person

This is the year of the gourd woman! She got up and went into her room. No longer the year of the would-like-to-be-slender woman, the wish-I-were-flat-chested woman . . . Cloe bears traces of her old skins. She is dappled, and walks giggling through the streets. Here and there, in the play of light and shadow, the variegated patches glow. The soft, ready-to-yield skin, the don't-be-so-oversensitive skin, the I-am-tranquility-personified skin, the sensual-curious skin, the want-to-experience-everything skin. Who can read a dappled skin?

Cloe moves her lips. I am my own woman. People turn and stare. To think that nowadays even young women have started talking to themselves!

Fiction is a passionate pleasure in many women's lives, far more so than it appears to be for men. Women, it seems, are addicted to fiction. As novelist Rachel Billington put it, 'Women read fiction. Women need fiction. Men do too but only the discerning. They read good novels. Women, even those with brains like razors, never lose that longing for the Big One, the big emotional high' (*Guardian*, 5 October 1981). And not only do women consume fiction, but novel writing is one of the few areas of the arts where women are recognized as equal to men.

It is not just novels in general that women consume. Recently a new genre of novel has appeared aimed at a specifically female audience and usually written by women. These are not just the novels of a publishing house like Mills and Boon specializing in romantic fiction for women; there are also more recent publishing ventures like Virago, committed to printing and reprinting books by women which are aimed at a female audience. Virago director Carmen Callil explained the commercial success of Virago as satisfying women's demand for women-centred fiction: 'We have shown there is a real public demand. We are looking for things in books which are central to women's experience' (*Guardian*, 26 January 1981).

The production of such novels where women's experiences are at the forefront and which are aimed at a specifically female readership is not, however, confined to the feminist press. The success for commercial publishers of novels like *Kinflicks*, *Original Sins*, *The Women's Room*, *The Bleeding Heart*, *Fear of Flying* and *The Woman Warrior* can hardly be overlooked. They have all at one time or another been hailed as 'the number one international best-seller'. And the success of these women writers, appealing with their women-orientated fiction to women, means that commercial publishers are looking out for more. Women *are* the fiction market. 'An English male writer in America was recently asked to use only his initials in order to disguise his unfashionable sex' (Billington, *Guardian*, op. cit.). What then is the history of these women-centred novels? What form of pleasure do they offer women and why have they become so popular now?

Women-centred novels are by no means a new phenomenon. Indeed, novels like *Pamela* and *Clarissa* are usually seen as the precursors of the modern novel and they had the lives of individual women at the centre of the narrative.[1] The novel as we know it today emerged as a distinct form of entertainment in the eighteenth century. It was a form of entertainment to be enjoyed in private, and at its heart was a narrative following the life of one individual. The novel, as an entertainment form, almost certainly emerged because the pleasures and interests which it offered corresponded to distinct historical conditions. Some think that the life and experiences of individuals came to the forefront in these stories at the same time as the values of the new bourgeoisie came to dominate social beliefs. The values of economic competitiveness and individualism, for instance – both crucial to the early novel – came into their own in this period.[2]

In the cases where a heroine occupied the position of central consciousness, the novel was invariably preoccupied with questions of sexual morality, and especially marriage. In fact novels increasingly featured the movement towards marriage as the centrally significant event of the narrative. The point of marriage was almost invariably the point where the narrative was resolved and often concluded. *How* that point was reached, of course, was all-important and varied enormously between writers. For Jane Austen, the movement towards marriage was invariably also a movement towards an intellectual apprehension of social values. For all the women protagonists in Jane Austen's novels, marriage represents the establishment of certain social values. In *Emma*, the sentimental lesson in the protagonist's appreciation of her love for Mr Knightley is also an intellectual lesson where her impulsive behaviour is criticized. In *Mansfield Park*, the marriage of Fanny represents the triumph of the established orders of the house Mansfield Park, upheld in the face of disintegration through new sexual, moral and economic forces.

Even though the progress and forms of the novels are quite different, it is still worth making some general points about marriage as a central narrative device. In most novels of this early period there is a crucial moment for the individual, embodied in the choices around marriage. For the individual heroine, it is a brief moment where *significant events may happen*, after which her choices and identity are lost for ever.

By the nineteenth century this narrative had become quite rigid, even though this is, of course, remembered as the period where the

[1] S. Richardson, *Pamela*, 1740–1; *Clarissa Harlowe*, 1746–7.
[2] See I. Watts, *The Rise of the Novel*, Chatto and Windus, 1957.

novel reached its greatest expression. In *Shirley*, Charlotte Brontë can write of her protagonist: 'Caroline was just eighteen years old and at eighteen the true narrative of life has yet to be commenced' – more accurate would be, 'the true narrative of the novel of this period'. For what is implicit is that the novel can justify this concentration on the consciousness of the heroine only around these moments of social and sexual decision. It is interesting to reflect that the consciousness of the heroine and her eventual marriage are dominant themes in the popular literature of the nineteenth century.

In retrospect, it is not so difficult to see why the 'heroine', her particular qualities and the decisions she took about marriage were so important for that period. One aspect shows this clearly. The female protagonists of the nineteenth-century novel are profoundly silent. Their characters express sensitivity and inner feelings. Their looks, as the saying goes, 'speak volumes'. Thus the same Caroline in *Shirley* speaks only through her appearance: 'her face expressive and gentle; her eyes were handsome, gifted at times with a winning beam that stole into the heart with a language that spoke to the affection'.

The female protagonists invariably hold the position of understanding; silently feeling, they naturally perceive and uphold what is truly valuable. As in Elizabeth Gaskell's *North and South*, the female protagonist in *Shirley* represents the soft and understanding aspects of humanity.

Women, then, were represented as somehow outside social relations. In both *Shirley* and *North and South*, the women are in some way untainted by the harsh world of economic competition which their lovers inhabit; they represent the realm of pure feeling. Indeed the heroines of this period do not even speak their desire and their love; they blush and their eyes are downcast. Theirs is a silent sexuality expressed again from the body, physically but without a voice.

Small wonder that women writers of this period had such difficulty with their female protagonists. Silent and subdued heroines didn't always suit the aspirations of women writers, who sometimes produced 'strange' atypical heroines such as Lucy in Charlotte Brontë's *Villette*. Lucy clearly experiences violent, if not pressing, sexual desire but cannot express it; the novel, for that matter, cannot speak it explicitly either. This violent desire does get expressed but in terms of what would now be taken to be a nervous breakdown and through the strange indentification Lucy feels with a neurotic, religious and sexually repressed teacher. *Villette*'s themes of derangement, fantasy and hallucination are typical themes which recur in other women writers of the period. Derangement and hallucination are responses to the burden of interiority placed on the heroine by the novel form, responses to the speaking silence of the female figure. Nor is it surprising to find women writers who followed this route and expressed this burden through their writings now rediscovered as the precursors of contemporary feminist writers.

In the nineteenth century, then, the consciousness of the heroine was treated in a recognizable format. Her choices were for a brief moment before marriage of crucial importance, socially and sexually. Yet she is the silent woman, necessarily silent and outside the cruelty and viciousness of the economic order. In retrospect we can now see how this novel form in fact corresponded to certain definite social ideologies. The marriage of this heroine whose sentiment and sensibilities put her above the economy provided a sort of validation of the social structure. Her love was somehow untainted and contributed very forcefully to the ideology which was able to separate the public, economic realm from the domestic. The domestic sphere could then be represented as the realm of pure feeling – borne by the woman – where men's true identity could be expressed. Novelistic conventions contributed to the rigid separation between the public economic sphere and the private domestic sphere. The ideology promoted within the novels allowed individuals to live at ease with their consciences; the ideology allowed them to believe that in loving a woman, a man expressed his true goodness. The ideology of the domestic sphere and the love of a good woman allowed people to treat their homes as if the economic world did not exist and as if individuals were not implicated in the injustice of this world.

This narrative structure dealing centrally with the heroine's marriage arose at a definite historical period and had distinct social reasons for existing. But in spite of historical changes, this kind of narrative still exists. Interestingly, though, it has moved to the margins, and is dismissed by the critics as pulp fiction. Pleasurable though this form of novel may be, it is a frozen and repetitive form, unable to lay claim to being serious literature because it no longer deals with the main problems of contemporary life. Contemporary romantic fiction is repetitive and predictable – speechless and pure heroine with a masterful and cruel lover whose better self is expressed in his love of the heroine. But it is no longer a form able to explore central social problems.

The *mainstream* of popular fiction, however, appears to have completely inverted the values of the Victorian novel. If Victorian heroines spoke only through their eyes and their central nervous systems, contemporary women protagonists are positively garrulous about their intimate personal histories. Everything must and can be told. ' "You must not tell anyone," my mother said, "what I am about to tell you," ' opens *The Woman Warrior*, and then proceeds to tell it all.[3] Contemporary woman-centred fiction is characterized by this; above all, the female protagonist has become the speaking sex.

If sexual desire rendered the Victorian heroine mad, it now appears to be a vital component of 'the number one international best-seller'. So much so, that 'women-centred' novels have become almost synonymous with the so-called sexual revolution. More than anything, the sexual revolution is presented as the transformation of women's relation to sex:

Liberating the libido. Getting sex straight was an essential first step along the noisy road to liberation; writing about it could be the next leap forward. Books by women surveying sex, and novels by women whose heroines savour sex, are selling like hotdogs in America – beating men into second place and turning authoresses into millionairesses at the drop of a hardsell dust-jacket.

Sunday Times Colour Supplement

These novels are often seen by the writers themselves as relating to feminism, although many feminists have received them with suspicion. Sometimes consciousness-raising is used as a narrative device, as in *Loose Change* and *The Women's Room*; often the encounter with feminism and the discovery of how general the individual's experience as a woman actually is, is a vital element of the narrative. But regardless of this political commitment, the commercial world has recognized these novels as a genre of sexual writing, showing that women can write about sex as well as if not better than men.

What then are we to think about these novels? What needs do they appear to satisfy? How did they arise and can they, as is sometimes claimed, 'change lives' and contribute to a more progressive understanding of women's sexuality?

One point which is immediately striking is that these novels have

[3] M. Hong Kingston, *The Woman Warrior*, Picador, 1981.

followed the general pattern in fiction towards sexual confession, a pattern already mentioned in 'Have You Tried Talking About It?' (see page 133). The confessional novel has become more and more dominant in contemporary fiction, both male and female. Increasingly the novel's structure has been based on the voice of the protagonist describing the significant events in his or her life. Since the turn of the century this stream of consciousness writing has been widespread. But recently, the consciousness has been more and more preoccupied with talking about sex. Sexual confessions moved to the mainstream in the 1950s and '60s with writers like J. D. Salinger, Kingsley Amis, Henry Miller and Philip Roth. These novels exhibit interesting similarities with Victorian pornography which took the form of detailed pseudo-autobiographical accounts of sexual encounters.[4] But it wasn't until the late 1960s that this kind of writing became virtually synonymous with women writers and sexual revolution.

Where the sexual confessions – both male and female – differ from their pornographic and romantic precedents is in the fact that the narrative has expanded to encompass a much wider span of significant moments. If the narrative of life was just beginning at eighteen for Charlotte Brontë's heroines, the contemporary heroine has met the crucial determinants of her life in the 'formative' encounters of childhood and adolescence. Childhood has become a period permeated with sexual meanings, foretastes and crucial moments in the development of sexual identity.

It is appropriate, too, that with this concentration on childhood should have come a peculiarly regressive form of writing. This form is the written equivalent of the family album. It has generated a convention where humorous sketches are delivered. 'Here's Aunt Emily. She married Uncle Morgan who ran off with the post-lady. They lived down White Bay Creek, and used to take in drifters.' Then follows the anecdote, the vignette to show just what type of person Uncle Morgan was. This often has the effect of reducing the characters to the bare bones of their particular eccentricity. And this form of writing is one of the reasons why many reviewers can't make up their minds whether they are dealing with a 'riproaring, hilarious' novel or something actually quite serious. Lisa Alther's *Kinflicks* is a novel which has met this fate. *Kinflicks* embodies a real tension in trying to make serious points about women's experience

[4] See, for example, Walter, *My Secret Life*, Granada, 1972.

in a form which is basically 'playing for laughs'. I call this style of writing regressive because it arises from an ideology of how children are supposed to see the world. The central protagonist is shown making sense of the world as a child makes sense of its world: children, it is believed, work out their world slowly, only through enquiry, eavesdropping, prying and looking into the closets of their immediate family. The child in this ideology is a sort of miniature detective, working out its genealogy, with a quick eye for the missing links.

This ideology also postulates that the child sees its world as essentially eccentric. All children, after all, believe that their family is more bizarre than the next one. And the ideology assumes that the child's view of its parents is extended to the whole world. The world is bizarre and eccentric, full of haphazard events, and occurrences which have no apparent causal connection. These novels about women's lives frequently attempt a re-creation of this childish world of eccentricities, anecdotes, and the sense of haphazard happenings.

Of course, this view of the world is a version of how reality is to the child. The lack of causal explanations, the haphazard events and inexplicable eccentricities are visions which, if they ever existed, are rarely carried into the adult world. In the adult world, a sense of the causal connection between things has been profoundly and irreversibly formed by that early history. In the adult world, strong feelings about how things happened are usually present. The adult blames and feels guilt, feels dependent on some people and rejects others, in short has taken up a place. This place is conditioned no doubt by infantile experiences, but these infantile experiences are now interpreted in the light of the adult personality. How indeed could a writer produce a 'true' narrative, in the sense of an objective account of events, not yet coloured by emotional dramas?

Yet these novels make their claim to a 'higher degree of realism' than their romantic predecessors precisely by attempting to produce an objective sequence of events and re-create a childish consciousness which does not see and does not evaluate the connections between people's actions. When it comes down to it, of course, even within this ideology the novels are making clear choices about what events are picked out as the most significant. In these novels where women's experience is highlighted, it has become a standing joke that we are to expect the first period, first kiss, first (fumbled) intercourse, first (disastrous) marriage, lesbian affair and usually lonely resolution. The end product is normally that the protagonist

feels she has 'become her own person'. This disingenuous construction of an adolescent world derives precisely from the novel's
attempt to create a higher realism. The complex family history and
interrelations, the anecdotes presented as if passed from generation
to generation, the eccentric view of the world, are all practices aimed
at creating the sense of the autobiographical. This is something
which is often reinforced by the way in which the central characters,
as in *The Women's Room* (Marilyn French) or *Sita* (Kate Millett), are
themselves writers or novelists.

It is no coincidence that high on the best-seller lists alongside
these 'novels that change lives' are the sexual autobiographies of so-
called personalities – Mandy Rice Davies, Joan Collins and Fiona
Richmond – who also employ these confessional tactics: family
genealogy, school days, first sexual encounters, then the hard stuff
of adult sexual experience. Women-centred novels represent a
fictionalized version of our culture's contemporary obsession with
autobiography and with intimate revelations.

Certain points can be made about the confessional forms of
writing and their preoccupation with sexuality. I have hinted that
this telling all does not in fact bear witness to a radical break with
our 'repressed' past. What used to be the structure of written
pornography has now appeared in the mainstream merged with the
traditions of the novelistic, derived from the heyday of the Victorian
novel. In fact, it has been suggested elsewhere that this obsessive
talking about sexuality represents a continuation of certain practices
relating to the control of sexuality. Sexuality in fact has never been
repressed as the vision of the Victorians would have it. For several
centuries now, sexuality has been at the heart of a number of
discourses, and since the last century has been made more and more
important. In the Victorian period, these discourses were directed
towards the prohibition of certain sexual practices, such as masturbation or female 'promiscuity'. We can see this negative aim in the
educational and medical writings of the Victorian era. But however
negative and controlling these discourses were, they all had sexuality as the central object of concern. In contemporary society there
has been a shift rather than a liberation in the treatment of sexuality;
now the discourses are directed at making sex explicit rather than
denying it.

In countries where the Catholic Church had a powerful presence,
the confessional seems to have influenced the form taken by these
social and scientific discourses on sex. Like church confessionals,

they simultaneously enquire into sexuality and command that all be revealed in its most minute and detailed ramifications. This detailed pursuit of the tiniest pleasures in sexuality was, of course, a method of control. Owning up to the pleasures of the flesh, the subject accepted the control of the Church, which was seen as having the key to the soul, bestowing forgiveness and absolution. Scientific discourses also 'listen' to sexuality *and* take sexuality to be the true expression of innermost identity. Hence pseudo-medical disciplines like sexology developed, classifying individuals according to their constitutional and sexual predisposition, anxious to fix and describe a whole classificatory system of sexualities. Michel Foucault, in *The History of Sexuality*, described the way in which power can be exercised through concern with sexuality. The identity of the subject is found within these discourses, which multiply the areas and possibilities for sexual pleasure only to control, classify and subject.

These ideas are useful because they indicate how the centrality of sexuality in novels, either coyly in romantic fiction or explicitly in confession of sexual experiences, has definite correspondences with the wider social organization of sexuality. We have to treat with suspicion the whole notion of sexual revolution which these novels are said to represent because there has been no such violent change from repression to freedom. Even the most apparently open and explicit detailing of sex can be an expression of sex in a way which means it is structured by very definite social·movements and relates to the structures of power in society at large.

Within the novel, the 'confession' has appeared overdetermined by traditions specific to the novel. In particular it has been influenced by the importance of narrative which organizes a series of events or experiences as significant and progressing towards a meaningful conclusion. This space of time, or narrative, is one in which the central character or characters undergo a series of experiences which radically affect their lives or transform their attitudes. The effect of this structure is to create a distinct ideology of knowledge and indeed life – that experience brings knowledge and possibly wisdom.

But where novels focusing on women's lives are concerned, a distinctive variant has occurred. Knowledge or understanding has been focused exclusively on sexual experience – love, marriage, divorce or just sexual encounters. This has the effect of reproducing the ideology where (albeit now disillusioned) women are viewed in relation to their sexual history. Women again defined through their sexuality, are the sex to be interrogated and understood. Becoming my own person or woman is in the grain of the sexual; it is how a woman deals with her sexuality. Novels with male characters may well also concentrate obsessively on sex. But what the sex means is different. For men, sexual encounters represent access to power, a series of encounters and experiences which build up a sense of the individual's power in having control over women's bodies. Sexual experience in women's novels represents access to knowledge, rather than power. Sexual experience becomes the way in which a woman finds out about herself.

There's a danger that such structures reproduce the Victorian ideology that sexuality is somehow outside social relations. The idea that a woman could become her own person just through sexual experience and the discovery of sexual needs and dislikes again establishes sexual relations as somehow separate from social structures. The emphasis on sex as knowledge may well obscure the fact that sex is implicated in society as a whole, that sex has consequences and that there are always other people to consider in a sexual experience. Questions of social responsibility and not hurting other people are no less important to women critical of conventional morality. Yet there's a danger that sexual experience has been represented as an end in itself, as if other social decisions and work experiences didn't affect us as much.

It is hardly surprising that women have been represented as having a crucial role in the 'sexual revolution'. We have already seen in 'Have You Tried Talking About It?' (see Page 133) how women's sexuality has been the prime site of the investigation of sexuality. Sexology, psychology, psychoanalysis, films, pornography all ask the question, 'What is women's sexuality?' It is not surprising that at a period when a society represents itself as shaking off the mysteries of our repressed past it is women who are represented as being at the centre of this transformation.

This society chooses to represent women as responsible for the sexual revolution: sexual repression was overthrown as soon as women were clear about wanting and needing sex as much as men. In fact, women have realized that greater freedom of opportunity for sexual intercourse does not in and of itself bring about changes in men's attitudes towards women, or changes in how the sexes relate to one another. Men, in short, have remained in their position of privilege, often contemptuous of women, who therefore did not gain from a discovery of their sexual personalities in the ways represented.

But does this invalidate these novels and their spoken commitment to changing the position of women? I think not. Because like
feminism itself, these novels probably transcend their origins in
wider social movements. It is not sufficient to suggest that because
women have been shot to the fore as the speaking sex they simply
reproduce the values which have made women the group whose
sexuality is interrogated. For as with the Victorian heroine, the
current preoccupation with women's sexual experiences corresponds
to a general social concern with women's social position and how it
will be resolved. Women's social position and possibilities have
changed radically in the last fifty years; conceptions of what is
possible and what is desirable have been greatly changed and such
changes represent upheavals to some of the most dearly held
ideologies and beliefs of this society. It would suit society to reduce
women to being *the* sex – the talking, the experiencing sex – because
again this would pose little threat to the idea of the experiential
individual at the heart of this society. But because women have
always been confined to this realm, albeit in different ways over
different historical periods, any investigation of this construction has
the potential for exposing it *as construction*. Thus even those novels
which appear to correspond to most widely held sexual ideologies
often attempt more interesting things. For the autobiographical
voice of these contemporary women-centred novels often appeals to
a collectivity. I am, but I am a representative of all women. The
history of my oppression is the history of all women's oppression.

And beyond the format are those writers who have begun to
deconstruct the whole notion of identity, at the same time challenging the conventions of the novel. Writers like Doris Lessing or Fay
Weldon both occasionally disrupt the conventions of a central
narrative voice or character, and their writing becomes a myriad of
historical, social and sexual concerns which do not belong to any
individual subjectivity. And both Doris Lessing and Angela Carter
explore the fantastic and the erotic in ways that do not appeal to any
realistic identification with a self-discovering heroine on the way to
her own personhood. Nor is it surprising to find reinstated other
earlier novelists who also stretch the reader's understanding beyond
the conventions of a sexual self-discovery. Some of Rosamond
Lehmann's novels, for instance, appear to explore the whole basis of
fiction, creating a narrative which can never be validated, where the
hopes and fantasies of the individual protagonists are validated and
the objective narrative rendered fictional.

The term 'women-centred' novels covers a multitude of sins. But at the heart of this multi-faceted phenomenon is one dominant convention, a type of narrative which corresponds to existing (and therefore problematic) ways of defining women through their sexual personhood. Because the whole issue of women's sexuality and changes in structures of living are crucial to our experiences now, these novels are sometimes able to explore the question of how female identity has been constructed and how this relates to society as a whole. Often, though, the convention itself pulls the novels back into banal repetitions, asserting a world without fantasy where women struggle on, often grim, brutalized and victimized. I'm not sure that becoming my own person is sufficient compensation for such a world.

An Overwhelming Desire

There must be thousands of women who subscribe to the opinion that Jane Austen's *Pride and Prejudice* has never been equalled as a romantic novel. Even now, centuries later, heterosexual and lesbian women alike secretly admit that the novel exemplifies all the necessary elements of a good romance. And heterosexual women also have been heard to admit that Mr Darcy takes some beating as a romantic hero.

Admittedly, *Pride and Prejudice*, being Literature with a capital L, has a rather rarefied appeal. But the ever-popular Mills and Boon novels are really not that dissimilar. The heroes of such novels are often endowed with Mr Darcy-like qualities: they are powerful in social position, scathing in conversation, distant in emotions and satanic in appearance. The *form* of popular romance is remarkably similar too.

Following a strikingly predictable and repetitive format any good popular romance has the following elements: a powerful hero, a heroine who is usually decent (though sometimes misled), and a number of difficult circumstances to be overcome before the happy resolution of the affair.

The narrative form of pulp romance is dominated by frustration. Marriage may be the goal to which the narrative slowly and surely progresses but the actual process of the story involves far more frustration than satisfaction. For a really good romance, there must be either some misjudgment by one or both of the protagonists, such as mistaking one another's character, or there must be almost overwhelming obstacles in the way of their getting together. The narrative structure revolves around obstacles, enigmas, and miscalculations. These only ever get resolved in the last few pages. The domineering hero overwhelms the heroine with his desire, but is also himself tamed by his love for this heroine. The frustrations encountered by the protagonists can be material: the result, say, of different class backgrounds. Or they can be caused by apparently incompatible characters, as when a basically good heroine or hero is misperceived by the other as bad, calculating or promiscuous. Frequently, there's another woman in the hero's life, usually more suited by background or lifestyle than our heroine.

No less than in these pulp romances, *Pride and Prejudice* progresses through obstacles, preconceptions, misconceptions, and embarrassments. Mr Darcy is 'above' marriage to Elizabeth Bennet but is gradually snared by his desire into what he sees as a 'shaming' proposition. This proposition offends more than it flatters and confirms Elizabeth's view of Mr Darcy as arrogant, presumptuous and cruel. The narrative is resolved only when the mutual misunderstandings have been removed, when Mr Darcy, in the throes of his overwhelming love for Elizabeth Bennet, has proved his worth and his power can be safely harnessed to hers in marriage.

In 'The True Story of How I Became My Own Person' (see page 173) I suggested that romantic novels were no longer the story form which investigated the significant social changes in women's lives. If this is the case, then how are we to account for the increasing popularity of romantic fiction, a popularity which has ensured that an organization such as Mills and Boon, along with the feminist publishing companies, is expanding through a recession? Charlotte Lamb, herself a romantic novelist, described the extent of this success:

> Over the past decade, the rise of feminism has been paralleled almost exactly by a mushroom growth in the popularity of romantic fiction. Last year alone 250 million women bought a Mills and Boon book, in countries ranging from France to Japan, from America to Australia.
>
> *Guardian*, 13 September 1982

Unresponsive though these novels may be to social changes, they must still satisfy some very definite needs. And in the repetitive formula, the predictable characters and the inevitable outcome, there is the evidence of a very powerful and common fantasy.

Let us take a closer look at the bare bones of this fantasy, the elements necessary to the characters and the form of the story. First there are the attributes of the hero. *His* characteristics are found in male protagonists across a number of media. Arrogance, power and social status are consistently offered up as attributes which women desire. Jack Nicholson, for instance, is 'forever sexy, for every reason – not least his fascinating flat voice and amused satanic eyebrows'. And in the film, *The Postman Always Rings Twice*, we can see Nicholson 'ravishing his co-star . . . A vicarious thrill from Jack is better than no thrill at all' (*Cosmopolitan*, November 1980). Power and dominance, if we are to believe the articles, are synonymous with sexiness in a man: 'my perfect male is the strong silent type with a dominant character' and 'He's the sexiest man around with an aura of power and strength that is almost touchable' (both quotes, *Sunday Times* Colour Supplement, November 1977).

And Paula Yates, a journalist who can always be relied on to give the most reactionary version of female views, sums up this ideology: 'I find men who have success, power and/or fame sexy . . . It's an appeal that dates back to Stone-age times when women naturally fell for the strongest man who was guaranteed to bring home the bacon' (*Cosmopolitan*, March 1982).

Attractive, desirable men in these kinds of fantasies are required to be 'charismatic', in other words to have certain socially agreed characteristics – power, dominance and social recognition itself. Interestingly, even current pop stars, who are often highly ambiguous in sexual presentation, are sufficiently endowed with the 'fame factor' to make them desirable. It would be relatively easy to account for these desirable attributes in a sociological way. After all, in this society fame equals wealth and cynics might say that financial advantage is the only reason for finding men attractive. It is certainly the case that the sexes tend to find attractive those very qualities which keep the relations of power as they are. But an understanding of fantasies purely from the point of view of the economic realities of men and women's lives gives us little access to the deeper realities which sustain these fantasies. Certainly the economic realities are important, but as an explanation they don't exhaust what's going on in these fantasies. Equally crucial is the fact that these fantasies about the adoration of male power have a curiously regressive quality. I don't mean politically regressive, although all the novels are exactly that; I mean regressive in the sense that the stories are directly reminiscent of infantile fantasies.

In the adoration of the powerful male, we have the adoration of the father by the small child. This adoration is based on the father as all-powerful, before disillusionment and the struggle for autonomy set in. Sometimes the patriarchal nature of the fantasy becomes explicit:

His words hit her physically, so forcibly did they remind her of her father: he had been the only person who had ever used that word to describe the colour of her hair. And now to hear Stephen do so – the man she loved, who could only see her as a machine – was more than she could bear. Eyes blinded by tears, she ran out.

Roberta Leigh

The way in which these men are portrayed certainly involves a journey back to a world before any struggle for autonomy has occurred. It isn't even an adolescent fantasy; it's pre-adolescent, very nearly pre-conscious. As a fantasy, it represents the adoration of a person on whom your welfare depends, the exaggerated evaluation which children experience before the process of becoming a separate person begins. As the child becomes more independent there's invariably a re-estimation of the parent, perhaps even a disillusionment. The parent who is no longer omnipotent in the child's welfare is no longer seen as omnipotent in the world. The child begins the difficult process of recognizing social valuation as well as personal valuation of the parents. The struggle for autonomy also brings its problems. By adolescence, there's usually a full-scale struggle for independence. Power which might previously have been adored – after all, it ensured the welfare of a dependent child – becomes controlling and suffocating for a child struggling to become independent. The power of one person is seen as depriving another of autonomy. Especially for women, the relationship to patriarchal authority is bound to be hazardous. Men have power and authority only if women's equality is denied.

But in the fantasies represented by these novels, the power of men is adored. The qualities desired are age, power, detachment, the control of other people's welfare. And the novels never really admit any criticism of this power. Occasionally the heroine's 'protest' their right to gainful employment, or rebel against the tyranny of the loved men. But in the end they succumb to that form of power. And what attracted them in the first place were precisely all the attributes of the unreconstructed patriarch. The qualities which make these men so desirable are, actually, the qualities which feminists have chosen to ridicule: power (the desire to dominate others); privilege (the exploitation of others); emotional distance (the inability to communicate); and singular love for the heroine (the inability to relate to anyone other than the sexual partner).

It is interesting to realize that obstacles do exist in the way of the heroine's adoration of her man. But the obstacles are never the criticisms or ambiguity which a woman might really feel towards that kind of man. The obstacles come from the outside, from material circumstances or misunderstandings. The work of the narrative is to remove these misunderstandings and obstacles, one by one. Instead of contradictory feelings towards such men, or feelings of suffocation, we have a number of frustrating circumstances which are finally cleared away to allow for the heroine safely to feel her respect and love for the man. In other words, these fantasies admit a belief that everything would be all right between the sexes were it not for a series of foolish misperceptions and misunderstandings.

There are a number of other factors which indicate a powerful infantile fantasy at work. For instance, there's the jealousy to which the heroine is invariably exposed. A rival for the hero's affections is almost obligatory, and the rival is usually better suited by class or by temperament. The crunch point in the narrative often comes when the heroine sees the hero and the other woman embracing, or meets the other two together. When the narrative is resolved, we discover that the hero was thinking about our heroine all along. He was either seeking consolation in another's arms, or was taken in by some scheming type. A satisfactory resolution of this obstacle is the discovery that the hero was after all loyal to the heroine, at least with the emotions if not the body.

The obliteration of a rival is another standard component of an infantile fantasy. The sight of the hero in another's arms is reminiscent of Freud's accounts of one of the forms taken by infantile jealousy provoked by the sight of the parents embracing. The child sees this and is jealous, seeking in fantasy to obliterate the intruding parent. Common childhood fantasies are of obliterating that parent and taking her/his place, becoming the rightful and only recipient of the other parent's love. In pulp romance, the disappointments based on discovering that others have claims on the loved one's attention are obliterated. There aren't really obstacles to total monomaniacal love, only temporary frustrations which the narrative then removes.

There is another significant way in which these narrative fantasies are regressive. It is the way in which sexual desire is portrayed. The hero's power is not only reminiscent of the father's perfection before the fall, so to speak; the power also works to absolve the women from any responsibility for the sexual engagement. Heroes are usually established as either sexually active (lots of girlfriends) or as almost untouchable. In the first case, the heroes are the objects of intense sexual interest, and have active sexual lives but refuse to settle down. In the end it is the overwhelming nature of their special desire for the heroine which is eventually secured. She alone has kindled the overwhelming desire that is going to end in marriage. The 'untouch-able' syndrome is really very similar. In these cases, the hero is remote, too good for sexual intrigue, better still a priest – somone, in short, who ought not to feel sexual passion. The heroine alone awakens his desire. The desire he feels for her is so great that he has to come off his pedestal, gather her in his arms and crush her to his chest.

All the frustrations and delays integral to a good romance only heighten this outcome, where the hero's desire is made suddenly explicit. The hero's desire is so great that it borders on the uncontrollable. One journalist called it the 'bruised lips' syndrome, and it is certainly the case that the uncontrollable desire has close resemblances with descriptions of rape. The heroine keeps her blouse buttoned up only with greatest difficulty until they can breathlessly mutter the marriage vows at each other and bring the novel to a satisfactory close: '"Please put your dress on," he murmured huskily, "so we can go talk to your parents about our wedding"' (Janet Dailey).

This fantasy is the ultimate expression of passive sexuality. The heroine may well be 'in love' with the hero. She may well adore him and admire him. But her *desire* is only ever triggered as a response, crushed out of her, as it were, as a series of low moans. Again psychoanalytic writing is illuminating about this kind of fantasy. It represents the projection of active desires by yourself on to another person, who then becomes responsible for that desire.

Freud suggested that amnesia about the events of earliest child-hood resulted from the repression of the active, masturbatory, usually incestuous desires felt by all children towards the people charged with the care of them. Hunger and the need for warmth and comfort are sensual satisfactions which become the basis of later sexual (specifically genital) satisfaction. And these sensations are stimulated initially by the person on whom the child is dependent. All children are expected to abandon this incestuous involvement with their parents but girls are also expected, in this society, to abandon the *active* sexuality characteristic of the infantile period. In patriarchal societies, the repression of active female sexual choice and activity is one of the ways in which women's subordination is secured. Thus as a girl child assumes a position in the adult world, a strong feeling of guilt is attached to infantile sexuality, however unconscious the experience may be. Sexuality has usually to be someone else's responsibility, not an activity desired by the female body and acted on and secured by the female person. Instead, female sexuality becomes centred on attracting, on making another person assume responsibility for women's desire.

The guilt women often feel about active sexuality is evidenced by the guilt which women seem frequently to feel about masturbation, a guilt apparently not shared by men. The pleasure is felt as somehow stolen, not quite right. This is probably because the activity is directly reminiscent of childhood sexuality – the organs and sensations are not necessarily those of the heterosexual act of penetration. It is therefore an activity which unavoidably reminds women of a sexuality outside the 'approved' act, and a sexuality for which only they are responsible.

In romantic fiction, however, sexuality is safely secured in the other person; actually another person who closely resembles the child's ideal father. All the elements in fact confirm this reading of a fantasy of parental seduction. The patriarch is all-powerful; he really only wants the heroine (favourite daughter); and his desire is so strong, so overwhelming that she can only respond. All obstacles which exist for this kind of love are cleared away; they are only the result of misunderstandings. In the end the father is restored to his 'original' position. He has total control but he is basically kind and will provide for her. Countless Mills and Boon novels end on this note of submission to male provision. Women give up their struggles for independence and autonomy. Their well-being is henceforth secured in the love of a great man.

One thing about these fantasies, though, is that however passive the female, she is not actually powerless. The conclusion of marriage isn't necessary so much for reasons of morality, but because these fantasies are very obviously about a certain transfer of power, from the man to the woman. The woman is not annihilated by her subordination to the patriarch; she also assumes some power over him since his great power is finally harnessed to one woman – the heroine. Indeed, there are often other elements in romantic novels where the men are rendered helpless and dependent, like children. There's often a scene where the hero falls ill, suffers from hallucinations in the desert, or is even injured:

The human frailty of Stephen Brandon's sickness – even though momentary – robbed Julia of her awesome fear with which she had regarded him. One could not see a man prostrate and not feel sorry for him; and sympathy – however fleeting – left change in its wake.

Roberta Leigh

Rendering the hero ill, dependent, or injured is a narrative device which crops up all over the place. There's a common theme in fiction and films of women being attracted to cripples, or having fantasies about nursing men through illnesses during which the man suddenly realizes that 'what he's been feeling is love'. Dick Francis's racing thrillers, which are extremely popular with women, have this theme of male mutilation down to a fine art. We can be sure that if the hero isn't brutalized within the first few pages, he'll certainly get shot, beaten up or fall off his horse pretty soon. Now, all this is extremely interesting; it points to a push for power in female fantasy.

In romantic fiction, the hero is made dependent only 'fleetingly', as Roberta Leigh would undoubtedly have it. But this momentary impotence allows the woman to acquire power, the power of a mother caring for a child. And the concluding marriage is the symbol of the woman achieving power. The men are castrated and then restored. The power which the heroine achieves is the power of the mother; the daughter has taken the mother's place.

The fantasies of romantic fiction are much more complex than representing women as licking the jack-boots of a nameless fascist (which is how domination is represented in the equivalent male fantasy in pornography). Women do acquire power in these fantasies. Men are injured, or are rendered the helpless slaves of passion. The great heart-breakers are brought into line and the proud and arrogant are apparently humbled by their sexual desire for the good heroine. This power, however, is always familial, always regressive. The potent father, the abolition of the rival mother, and taking the mother's place are the classic structures of childhood fantasy in a nuclear patriarchal family. It is a fantasy that maintains men as actually powerful, 'out there in the world', and maintains women as passive, gaining their power only through their relations with men/ children. The fantasy secures women's desire *for* a form of heterosexual domination and *against* active sexual identity.

Romantic fiction is surely popular because it manages to restore this fantasy against all the evidence. It restores the childhood world of sexual relations and suppresses criticisms of the inadequacy of men, the suffocation of the family, or the damage inflicted by patriarchal power. Yet it simultaneously manages to avoid the guilt and fear which might come from that childhood world. Sexuality is defined firmly as the father's responsibility, and fear of suffocation is overcome because women achieve a sort of power in romantic fiction. Romantic fiction promises a secure world, promises that there will be safety with dependence, that there will be power with subordination.

The Story

Following a story, be it in a novel, a film or on TV, is always some sort of escape from reality. Any story offers a slightly different version of reality from our own. And some stories offer escape into totally different worlds, into fantastic and bizarre happenings or at least into situations completely different from our own lives. The unfolding of a narrative offers some of our most pleasurable experiences. But not all the stories available to us come from books or the screen; some of the richest stories are in our own heads. They come from the life of fantasy.

Fantasy is the 'other place' of the mind. Fantasy is like a secret room or garden, to be visited in a spare moment. Many women talk of looking forward to the moment of escape when they can enter the rich and creative world of their own minds, hidden from the rest of the world. In 'the other place', real situations can be visited, replayed, perhaps differently. New meanings or intentions can be given to the words and actions of other people; the bare bones of daily social intercourse can be fleshed out into a Wagnerian epic.

In fantasy you can create new people in your life, invent new lovers and put yourself through all sorts of novel experiences. Your children can be given all sorts of bizarre and elaborate futures. You can achieve all manner of things, trying out life as a film star, a female jockey, a contented mother. In the world of fantasy, you can safely destroy your life, put your friends, lovers and parents in mortal peril, and then rescue them. Sometimes you don't. Fantasy is like a trip to the local cinema. The decor is familiar, so is the feel of the seats, but the films are different – albeit slightly – each time.

Fantasy is different from dreaming proper. We tend to impose narrative coherence on dreams only when we wake up, because the activity of dreaming is different from the activity of waking thought. In dreams some thoughts are condensed into one image, or then again one image may stand in for another. In this way dreaming allows the expression of unconscious wishes without this being recognized by the conscious mind. Thus you might dream about a distant acquaintance named Ann and be puzzled why. Later you may remember that Ann is also your mother's name, and then the dream might make more sense. On waking the dreamer tries to put the images together into a sequence, like a narrative, when in fact the images are linked by associations rather than casual or logical connections.

Fantasy is more like day-dreaming. Fantasy has to satisfy the watchfulness of the conscious mind, not producing any material which is likely to displease this fierce censor. Narrative, in fact, is something of a signal that secondary revision has taken place, that events have been strung together in a way that satisfies the requirements of the conscious mind in our culture: this happened, then this, the outcome was this, and the world said . . . The true dream has a wonderful way of avoiding such causal explanations, of putting all sorts of bizarre people in unlikely situations without so much as a nod at plausibility. The dream makes use of the richness of language and words; dreams use ambiguity in images, words and names in order to express unconscious wishes and fears. The conscious mind doesn't necessarily recognize that a fast one has been pulled. The dreamer is left with the images, wondering what, for example, the ticket collector was doing weeding her back garden.

With fantasy, however, the conscious mind is there like a watch-dog, anxious to put things together with a sense of cause and outcome and to do it in such a way that the wish expressed doesn't come into direct conflict with social values. Mind you, there are different levels of fantasy and some are much more like dreaming proper. The 'most conscious' fantasy is like day-dreaming and has most in common with the novel. This kind of fantasy tends to stay quite close to 'reality', reworking existing situations, creating new but plausible scenarios, or inventing stories around sexual and public ambitions. These fantasies can usually be controlled. But sometimes unwelcome material crops up. Many people describe how they give way to a pleasurable fantasy which then has to be restarted if unwanted images appear. Here's a character in a novel having this kind of experience:

If she goes on like this, what with her ethereal pallor, her caved-in stomach, slender limbs, her hair grown long and bleached from letting it float behind her as she swims, she will have become physically unrecognizable. What a shock for him when he appears: for, since he has neither telegraphed nor written, appear he surely must: any day, any moment now. He will alight from a specially chartered biplane . . . No, no, of course not, he loathes flying . . . One of the little steamers that ply between the islands will land him one morning or one evening. She will stand still while he walks towards her slowly with a white set face. He will catch his breath and murmur: 'I had to come. I've missed you day and night. Is it really you? You've changed.'
'Yes I've changed. You have come too late.'
'Too late? You mean you can't forgive me?'
'I mean I don't love you any more.'
Will he believe it? Not he, he's too conceited. A painful scene ensues, at the

end of which he slinks away, accepting his dismissal. Next moment back he strides, masterful, passionate, won't take no for an answer, pulls out all the stops.

And then . . . and then? The great scene of reconciliation will not build itself. Alien material keeps intruding.

Rosamond Lehmann, *A Sea-Grape Tree*, p.65

Other fantasies are somehow more persistent than the stories we tell ourselves, the pleasurable reconstructions of our situation. Little stories or scenarios can crop up which are almost involuntary. They can be pleasurable or actually disturbing. A common example is the persistent fantasy of what society defines as 'perverse' sex, for instance homosexual fantasy. For many people rooted in hetero-sexual prejudices, such an image can be intensely disturbing, as it appears to indicate that they have desire of a kind of which this society disapproves. Another example is the death scene, involving yourself or people you love. Again, this is often hugely disturbing. If I imagine my own death, am I dangerously suicidal? If I suddenly imagine the death of a friend, am I wicked? A murderer? In these involuntary fantasies, unconscious thoughts and wishes are intruding into our more conscious thought processes; the image persists and calls out for attention.

There's another level of fantasy as well, the kind where we start mistaking other people's actions and seriously misjudging events around us. In a persecution fantasy, for example, everyone is attributed with hostile and aggressive intentions. Freud suggested that this kind of fantasy sometimes resulted from the subject's own aggressive intentions. Rather than admit aggression towards a particular person or situation, that aggression is projected on to other people. Jealousy too can sometimes acquire 'fantastic' qual-ities. Exceeding even the understandable fears connected with uncommunicative partners, jealousy sometimes takes the form of putting lovers in complicated and elaborate scenarios which then cause intense unhappiness. Whatever the cause for such fantasies – desire for more active sexual involvement yourself, repressed homosexuality, or the repetition of a fantasy of abandonment in childhood – these are the kind which can barely be controlled, which haunt and upset the person who has them.

When daytime fantasies disturb in this way, they are doubtless expressing unconscious material. On the whole, though, fantasies tend to be compromised. By this I mean that they can satisfy unconscious desires without running into trouble with a very deep, socially constructed sense of what is acceptable. All fantasies are intensely private. Witness how embarrassed people are about relating their fantasies. So somewhere along the line, the stories in our heads are thought to be appropriately private, expressing parts of ourselves which we'd rather keep quiet. But most fantasies manage to avoid conflict with deeply held conscious beliefs about who we are, how good we are, how much we love our parents, and what kind of sex we like. When fantasies begin to defy these beliefs too persistently, 'neurotic' behaviour can result – those who try hard to put a stop to the inner life of fantasy find that it starts expressing itself wherever it can.

Some fantasies, however, are not private; they are the fantasies of a given society. Christianity for example has all the characteristics of a complex fantasy: there's the virginal mother, the powerful and distant father attacked by a malicious individual (the devil), and a son put through gruesome torture, dead but not really dead. These are the unconscious preoccupations of a patriarchal culture expressed in an acceptable way. Novels, films, TV narratives are all also various forms of public fantasies. Their writers and creators are just people who make their fantasies public and perhaps more elaborate.

Acts of public fantasy are interestingly marked by sexual characteristics. Women don't seem to like the same kinds of fantasies as men. War films, 'chaps-against-the-elements' stories, or violent thrillers are all received as completely uninteresting to most women. We just don't find them pleasurable. Clearly however, these are fantasies in which men can lose themselves, and they appeal to certain preoccupations of the male psyche. Apart from the sheer level of aggression and competitiveness, the kind of narratives which men enjoy are preoccupied with putting the male body through all sorts of ordeals; heroic endeavours up heretofore unscaled peaks, solitary survival in the Antarctic with but a string vest to wear, endurance in the face of war's carnage – these are the necessary components of a good male yarn. Crucial to these stories is the phenomenon that, somehow, one body – usually the hero's – comes through the carnage *intact*. It doesn't matter if the odd limb is blasted off, the odd eye lost; so long as the hero gets his girl or social recognition, he remains intact. He's a man.

These public fantasies seem to work over a preoccupation with castration. Men expose themselves to threats and ordeals which are ultimately survived. These themes are often encapsulated in the final image: hunky hero, mission completed, all washed up on a beach or similar with the faint sound of rescue coming into earshot. Survival against the odds suggests these fantasies are a sort of compromise between fear of castration and wish-fulfilment for the invulnerable body. Car chases, which leave the average woman cold, seem to confirm this theory. The car is chased, shot at, crashed into, run into, overturned, crushed, and usually written off. The hero, though, generally comes out with only a few wounds. The car is obviously some kind of symbol for the body. It is submitted to attacks and wounds but the hero pulls through. Morality doesn't enter into this kind of fantasy. It makes not the slightest difference whether the hero is a cop or a robber. He's an entire man.

These narratives give us some kind of idea about how narratives in general operate. The 'identification' which the reader or viewer makes is not necessarily with the hero/heroine or star but with the story. It is the anticipation of satisfaction from the story/fantasy that holds our attention, not some identification with a particular character. Socially sanctioned acts of fantasy often confirm dominant social attitudes. So, the male fantasies of violence validate taking risks and acting aggressively; after all, a power-through-invulnerability will be conferred by survival. What is more, these fantasies eschew the real possibility of vulnerability and celebrate power.

It is really interesting to see how women react to male fantasies. On the whole we switch off, get on with the ironing while the chaps race over the roof tops. But if we stop and watch, we can be really shocked. Men don't really like that stuff, do they? It's unnerving to think that a partner might be having imaginary shoot-outs and punch-ups, dropping the odd bomb, when he's meant to be doing the washing up. There are numerous accounts of women 'discovering' pornography amongst their lover's possessions. They describe the experience of 'creepiness' in thinking that their mild man is imagining a hundred and one ways to subdue a woman.

Of course, these public fantasies are only one side of the story; they are fantasies which do not challenge the dominant views about how society should operate. Publicly sanctioned fantasies confirm men's power, women's subordination. But we should be careful not to confuse the publicly approved with the fantasy life of the individual. Obviously there are correspondences. Public fantasies display for us a model of how to imagine and satisfy preoccupations central to the general forms taken by masculinity and femininity in

this society. But all those little tales which we're so unwilling to
share with each other also tell a different story. Here we have all the
wild, wilful and perverse qualities of the imagination; here we
commit murders and passionate adultery; here we achieve things
and succeed. Even the most 'feminine' fantasies express these
'masculine' attributes. Just take the fantasy described by Rosamond
Lehmann which I quoted earlier. This is a classic female fantasy – a
jilted woman dreams of her lover's return. It is 'female' in the sense
that the lover returns presumably overwhelmed by his desire for her;
he can no longer live without her. And this is indeed the supposed
outcome of the fantasy; the woman responds to the overwhelming
desire. But in the course of the fantasy, the woman takes up what
can only be described as a 'masculine' position. She fantasizes about
revenge and punishment; she dreams about rejecting him and
getting her revenge, the ultimate revenge – 'I don't love you any
more.' And the fantasy involves, like romance, immense power. The
man, although powerful, is humbled and controlled. It is a dated
view of sexuality but it gives us a good insight into how, in
individual fantasy life, the positions of masculine and feminine are
much less clearly fixed. Even when women fantasize about success
through other people – husband or children – they are, in fact,
investing in a fantasy of power and success. It is often precisely the
'masculine' and 'immoral' attributes of persistent fantasies which
disturb women who have been conditioned to think that they should
subordinate desires and ambitions to the constraints of patriarchal
culture.

Perhaps this is the reason why you often hear women expressing
the desire to 'escape' from their own thoughts – better to go out to a
film or pick up a book rather than to submit to the stories in your
own head. At least public entertainment offers a relatively fixed
cosmology; there, on the whole, women are women and men are
men. In the private life of the mind, nothing is certain, nothing is
fixed.

PART V

THE INSTINCT

The Sex-life Of Stick Insects

For as long as I can remember, David Attenborough has been in my living-room showing me the delights and wonders of nature. When I was a small child he used to show me nature as an infinite variety of exotic species. While I stayed at home he went everywhere, an intrepid traveller struggling through swamps and cutting back the tendrils on jungle plants just so I should know about birds of Paradise and the strange life of the Galapagos Islands. In the fifties and sixties, nature used to be a series of marvels brought to us by bold and eccentric travellers. Each week we would watch transfixed as Armand and Michaela Denis risked all with the rhinoceroses and Hans and Lotte Hass tempted fate among the sharks.

Nature seems to have undergone a bit of a transformation since then. Nature is even more popular on television. The programmes are prestigious, aimed at international audiences and guaranteed huge viewing figures at home. But nature is no longer an array of exotic and novel sights brought to us by eccentric and knowledge-able travellers. Instead, the activities of nature – the minute transformations of the organisms, the reproduction of the species and the processes of the seasons – have moved into close-up. And David Attenborough is usually relegated to voice-over, his dulcet tones employed to describe the natural processes – the perils of drought, the coming of the rains, the risky business of egg-laying, the relief and renewal when spring arrives.

The voices of David Attenborough and his like will tell us about a world of seasonal patterns, of the interdependence of species, of dangers, survivals and renewals. And while the gentle voices lull us, the exquisite photography unfolds before our eyes – close-ups of humming-birds on the wing, of flowers devouring insects, of worms cloning in compost heaps. But most especially, at the heart of all good nature programmes, is a privileged sight: mating. Whatever the subject, be it the ecology of a pond, a mountain orchid, or the life-cycle of the newt, we can be sure of one thing: at the end of the programme we'll know all about how they do it. Nature in the seventies and eighties has turned into a stunning sex show. In glorious colour and lingering detail, we can watch elephants copu-lating, fishes ejaculating, and the ritual courtship of the crested

---

* All the quotations in this piece come from one of the following: 'Wildlife on One' series – The Passing of the Black Buck; The Dragon and the Damsel. 'World About Us' – The Great Barrier Reef; Close Encounters of the Floral Kind.

grebe. The whole nation held its breath one Sunday evening when the pencil-thin penis of a whale was brought to the surface.

Natural history programmes have a great deal to say about sexual characteristics and sexual behaviour and without it being explicit, what they say can be applied to human society. Without appearing to do so, natural history programmes have implications for the understanding of human society in general. Nature programmes offer general explanations about how phenomena and organisms relate to one another, explanations which are startlingly absent from just about any other form of TV entertainment. So anxious is British television not to be accused of 'being political' that it is rare for a programme to offer general hypotheses about how social institutions and groups relate to one another. There are numerous separate investigations – into the steel industry, genital herpes or unemployment in the North West – but there's rarely any explicit hypothesis of how aspects of society relate to one another. Yet the question of how and why divisions arise between sexes, races and classes are surely just as pressing as why the female mantis eats her partner while mating?

Natural history programmes are able to address general questions about how separate phenomena relate – how the pond snail relates to the weeds, for instance. But while appearing to confine themselves to the life of beasts and plants, the programmes offer consistent comment on human society. This comment is not the demagogic, unscientific, obvious sort of comment such as those made by the likes of Desmond Morris. Instead, the programmes draw often unstated analogies, leaving the viewer to make the connections. Typical in this approach was a 'World About Us' programme on the Great Barrier Reef. After describing the complex interdependence of all the creatures, the programme concluded with a warning: 'there's a new animal in the reef: man. Can the reef accommodate this new life? Can it survive the activities of man? After all, we haven't evolved together.' We are left in little doubt here that man is man among the other animals, a hypothesis which is never very far away.

Two explanations of how species relate in the natural order dominate natural history programmes. The first offers nature as a variety of inter-relating species, each of which has evolved in a relation of complex dependence on the others around it. We are told about the 'design features' of each species, how these features connect with patterns of other species: 'both humming-birds and such flowers are vital to one another's survival'. We are shown how tiny aspects in the life-cycle of one species are vital to the life of another species. Each plant and animal is complexly dependent on the activities of another: 'Birds feed in surrounding waters, and their droppings enrich the sand, readying it for the arrival of seeds floating in on the tide, borne by the winds or carried in on the feet of yet other birds.' We are shown how 'insects making preparation for their own mating unwittingly become entangled in a floral encounter'. In these accounts everything fits together, perfectly, and the camera reveals how. The perfection of nature is matched only by the perfect design of the camera: 'Far beyond the normal limits of the eye, each grain of pollen is a masterpiece of design, its surface sculpture as individual as a fingerprint – different pattern, different species. It must fit the female stigma as precisely as a key fits a lock.'

These accounts of nature are of nature as a cycle, of seasons mellowing and plants dying, of dormancy and renewal. Everything has a purpose in this natural cycle, even destructive behaviour. Parrot fishes, we are told, are major herbivores of the Barrier Reef. They take out large lumps of the coral as they bite and scrape at the weeds: 'They are a destructive force but they are part of the natural process of growth, destruction and consolidation that builds a reef.' No less, the Bush fires of Western Australia: these 'may seem a totally destructive force but in fact, they are essential to the reproduction of certain plants'. And here we have it. At the heart of this wonderful and perfect process lies the ultimate mechanism of renewal: reproduction.

These programmes celebrating nature as a perfectly designed, functioning totality are in fact more in vogue currently than the other major type of nature programme: the survival programme. The survival programme is more likely to emphasize the bloody side of nature, giving graphic close-ups of honey possums munching their way through butterflies. Here nature is very much 'red in tooth and claw'. Species struggle against species for their right to survive. Mating on the whole takes second place besides pictures of eagles ripping apart snakes and feeding them to their voracious young. Both types of programme emphasize the precariousness of life and, at the same time, the miracle of life – a dangerous and wondrous cycle, sustained by sex.

Whatever the programme, however, it is certain that reproduction will be a central focus. Ritual courtship, mating and offspring will always be crucial. 'How do they have sex?' is a question asked even of the floral and insect world, providing us with a naturalist's *Kama*

Sutra. Dragonflies, for instance, have a 'unique' practice: 'Most insects mate tail to tail but male dragonflies have a second set of sex organs underneath their bodies. The male transfers sperm from his tail to this secondary organ. The female bends her tail round to make contact with it and the pair assumes a bizarre and characteristic wheel position.' Unfortunately, these programmes do not content themselves with the singularity of the mating habits of species. Instead, they never miss a chance to tell us about the sexual characteristics of the male and female of the species. We encounter, with monotonous regularity, the 'dominant' male defending his 'territory'; the hierarchies between males in their access to females; the existence of harems. We hear of females (and young males) assuming submissive postures. And we hear endless examples of home-making and parental provision.

Here in the animal kingdom, a natural world of male dominance and aggression is revealed. Here are males defending their property (territory and wives). Here are females selecting their mates as 'good' parents, either for their genetic endowments or their ability to provide. Over one tenth of black bucks, for instance, are territorial. They mark their territories with piles of dung and sit on them most of the day. When they go to drink they come into conflict with other males, sitting on their piles of dung. 'Conflicts ensue', at first minor ones, but becoming serious as the rut begins. The rut escalates conflict because 'more bachelor males' try and set up territories and 'unlike fights between established holders, fights between bachelor males and territory holders can be prolonged and violent'. In passing we learn that the harem-like appearance of the black buck's lifestyle is only an appearance, and that the mother only periodically visits her new-born calf. Nevertheless little is made of these minor details in comparison with the great weight of evidence of male territoriality and dominance. The overwhelming impression of such a programme confirms rather than contradicts the assumptions made in this society about male and female behaviour.

The examples of this kind are endless. At breeding time among the fishes, we are told that 'There's a good deal of fighting and aggressive display as the various fish defend their particular patch of breeding ground. The males at this stage are very aggressive indeed.' Even the dragonflies are endowed with the attributes of a dominant male, in relentless pursuit of a receptacle: 'in most species mating has little preliminary. This female is unreceptive but with another, the male has more success. The male seizes the female behind the neck with a pair of claspers at the end of his tail.' Everywhere in the natural world, there appears to be male rivalry, aggression, and a male determination to scatter seed wherever and whenever. 'Mating may last for several minutes and during this time the male may remove any rival sperm before inserting his own.' The interesting sex life of the female, which may have led to this situation, is passed over without comment.

Opportunities are rarely missed to remind us of natural hierarchies. There's usually a dominant male, and rivals waiting on the periphery longing to get in on the act. These males are intensely property-conscious, escalating conflict when they are the 'owners' of territory. They also respect leadership. Bison, it is hinted, were asking for extinction on account of 'their weak leadership situation'.

These popular programmes are on the whole fed by evolutionary theories. I don't wish to take issue with such theories, nor the possibility that there may be a certain continuum between animals and humanity. What worries me about the programmes is that they often *assume* as much as they *explain*. In some minds there are aspects of evolutionary theory which still require explanation – in particular how and why sexual differences arise since sexual reproduction is not strictly necessary.

But many of these programmes set out with a whole series of preconceptions about male and female behaviour; they take a whole baggage of preconceptions about male aggression, bachelorhood, dominance, property, women's nesting instincts. Indeed, these programmes are often intensely anthropomorphic, by which I mean that all sorts of human and social attributes are projected on to the behaviour of animals. The language used, the kind of background music used and the activities described are often couched in intensely human terms. The whole issue of how human behaviour resembles animal behaviour is intensely complicated, one that clearly requires scientific investigation. But often these programmes elude the problems, assuming that human meanings of 'father', 'mother', 'property' or 'home' can just be transferred on to the animals.

The projection of social and human values on to animals is something which has gone on for as long as nature has been studied. Interestingly, this point was made in 'The Study of Animal Behaviour', an excellent natural history series which showed how assumptions about animal behaviour have tended to reflect the concerns of the society which produced them as much as objective scientific investigation. And the assumption which comes through most forcibly in current investigations of nature is the rigidity of sexual divisions. This is why mating has such a central place, since it is the coupling of the two sexes and allows concentration on different behaviour patterns. It is extremely rare for programmes to empha- size the 'perversity of nature', or to emphasize routine social activities. It is rare for the programmes to comment on female groups as anything other than 'harems'. Who is to say that these are not primarily female groups which have marginalized males, except one good-looker tolerated for his reproductive function?

Some of the more 'scientific' programmes which set out to investigate sex are investigations which are also loaded with assumptions about sexual difference and what this means. One programme which showed how all foetuses start life as females was entitled 'The Fight to be Male', a title which left us in little doubt as to which was the more vigorous and advanced sex. And a pro- gramme about the 'Miracle of Life', which showed a sperm's-eye- view of conception, managed to endow sperms and ova with 'masculine' and 'feminine' characteristics. We were treated to a sight of the 'sperm armada' going to battle, and a display of male bonding as the lads helped the 'successful' sperm make his conquest.

In the nineteenth century, there was a vogue among 'social scientists' for examining other human societies in order to discover universal truths about the human species. Non-European societies were on the whole seen as primitive versions of our own society; in these societies, the scientists believed, it would be possible to see humanity in its earliest forms. The subject which particularly preoccupied investigators in this period was the question of mar- riage forms. In particular, the question asked of these other societies was, did they provide evidence for the universality of the patriarchal family, that is, the family recognizing male dominance and succes- sion through the father's line?[2] In fact, several of the societies studied revealed interestingly 'perverse' variations; in some societies, descent was reckoned through the mother's line rather than the father's. Debate about these phenomena was fierce, though on the whole most theorists were agreed that these perverse societies were either degenerate or represented the very first forms of human society – patriarchy in both cases being the civilized outcome.

It took serious study within the field of anthropology, and strong criticisms of this kind of social evolutionism, to reveal that such

[2] For an account of these debates see my earlier book: R. Coward, *Patriarchal Precedents*, Routledge and Kegan Paul, 1983.

deductions about the history of human marriage were in fact built on racist and imperialist presumptions rather than on scientific study. It took time to establish the fact that if different societies did not all respect patriarchal forms, they had different reasons for their social institutions and weren't simply primitive versions of Western forms.

These nineteenth-century debates, in retrospect, can be seen to have been based on an obsession with the way in which sexual relations were ordered, and how these related to society as a whole. They were particularly concerned with marriage, family, and property rights. It seems that the contemporary obsession is proving the inevitability of sexual difference rather than proving the universality of one family form. The contemporary obsession takes the form of repeating time and time again how sex (understood as mating) is necessary to the process of life, and how sex is premised on one sex being radically different (and perhaps by implication superior) to the other: 'although sex is not the only way of reproduction, nature has preserved it in both plant and animals as a way of increasing variety and vigour in offspring and hastening the on-going slow-explosion that is evolution'. How useful it is that nature delivers up this message; how gratifying that possessiveness, dominance and aggression can all be found in nature as part of the process of evolution. It would be too bad, wouldn't it, if nature made us question how we treat each other, and challenge what humans do to each other in the name of profit and power?

Affairs of the Heart
Are Well-aspected

Horoscopes are a fixed reference point in most leisure magazines; they even turn up in newspapers. We all turn to them with but a single question: 'What's going to happen to me?' Horoscopes generate that comfortable sense that someone knows the answer to that question. Someone somewhere is thinking about you, knows all about your character, and can tell what's coming. Doubtless this is why horoscopes continue to be written and why we continue to read them, even if it is with a large pinch of salt.

In this so-called rational universe, we are supposed to look to science for explanations. We aren't meant to believe in ghosts and spirits, astral bodies and the like. But here in the horoscopes we have an ancient world of superstitions. Here we have beliefs like those of the Middle Ages; here we have character determined by the position of the stars and fates decided by the movement of the planets. In the distant beyond, our lives are charted out as the stars whirl through the universe, moving in and out of each other's paths.

With the movements of the stars come a train of familiar events. They don't cause revolutions or strange unnatural happenings – two-headed births or monsters stalking the streets of the home counties. Instead the stars move familiar little things about. Stars affect lives like someone tidying a room, moving elements around within definite parameters. Some things get thrown away or lost; new arrangements are made, but the room remains the same. Today we might expect a windfall; we might meet someone from our past; or we may have to expect a bout of uncommunicativeness from a partner.

Vague though the formulations are – 'Some sort of family arrangement will be put into effect today'[1] – the range of events which concern the stars is surprisingly small. The actions of the stars bring with them a series of precise events in a limited field of action: domestic or personal affairs, atmosphere and advances at work, finances, and travel. Stars influence affairs of the heart: 'An angular planetary picture over the weekend will ... bring the chance to repair a broken relationship.' Stars also regulate the domestic temperature: 'February promises a great sense of release from any domestic tensions you've been undergoing in recent months.' The

[1] This and all subsequent quotations come from one of the following horoscopes: Patric Walker in the *Standard*, Circe in *Cosmopolitan*, Jillie Collings in *Woman*, Carole Golder in *Living*, Orion in the *Daily Mail*.

stars are very interested in careers, and especially the state of your ambition: 'The coming year will be an exciting one as far as your career and ambitions are concerned.' They also watch over journeys, warning rather ominously: 'Travel. Take care on Monday.' And they take a close interest in the state of your finances, recommending caution, economies or giving their blessing to long-held plans. Astral bodies have a deep concern with something they call partnerships: 'a partnership may be proving intractable'; 'It looks as though you'll be preoccupied with trying to sort out both partnership and professional matters'; and 'slow-moving planets do seem to indicate that a joint financial arrangement now being discussed may not be to your advantage in the long term'.

Roland Barthes, describing the horoscopes in *Elle* magazine in the 1950s, noted how the astral bodies didn't open up a dream world, a world beyond our daily life. On the contrary, the horoscope merely mirrored the social world of the readership. The stars observed the conventions of the *petit bourgeois* lifestyle, watching over the working week, obedient to social institutions and conventions, and expecting visits from the family at the weekend. The astral bodies even entered into the prejudices of this world, threatening trouble from the in-laws 'who the stars don't seem to hold in very high esteem' (R. Barthes, *Mythologies*). The pseudo-science of the horoscopes, in short, mirrors the social reality of the group producing them. This observation still holds true. Sexual adventure may have become a little more complex, and social occasions may have broadened out a little beyond the family, but while the stars may shift in their tracks, the life of society remains remarkably still: the institutions of romance, family, wages from the boss, windfalls and investments have hardly moved at all.

What happens to us within the limits of the status quo is determined by 'luck'; things go well if the stars are well-aspected or if there's a benign planetary influence in our charts. To most of us, the 'science' of these charts could just as well be in Chinese. Who after all understands the implications of 'There's not a single planet in the lower half of your solar horoscope at the moment, everything's way up at the top. And after September 8, either in Virgo, Libra, Scorpio or Sagittarius'? The planets could just as well be in Aquarius or Aries; we don't care so long as we find out whether a new relationship is due this week some time.

Very few people care about the pseudo-science of astrology. But lots of people are interested in whether they are going to strike lucky.

Lots of people are interested in whether something good is going to happen: are they going to win the pools, get a promotion, find a job? Among the stars such events are determined by chance, the accidental movement of astral bodies. Against rationality; against forms of causal explanation which might put you at the centre of your actions; and against the fact that the political choices of others determine your life, horoscopes feed an ideology of the passivity of the individual in the face of a fate which is already decided.

The classification of individuals into character-types is the other great function of astrology. This classification also feeds the ideology of individual passivity. Responses which are 'in keeping' with the characters of our birth sign are the only freedoms which exist for us in the horoscope world. Gemini's inventiveness and two-sided character will carry her through a tricky situation. Cancer's home-loving and tenacious character will get her into trouble in a difficult relationship. The extroversion of a Sagittarian means she can make the best of broadening social horizons. Taurean girls have to be careful not to be too stubborn. Ariens ought to watch out not to be too demanding.

Here we have the whole cosmology of character-types which would explain away the conflicts and difficulties which we might encounter in this kind of society.

Astrology conforms to, rather than creates, an explanation of character which predominates in Western capitalist society, according to which people have set characteristics which determine how society works. Either a person is stubborn or yielding, tough or gentle, creative or practical, demanding or supportive, conformist or non-conformist. And so the list goes on. These characteristics are in turn supposed to explain conflicts between people and the way things are – why some people are leaders and why others are born to follow. Here's a typical astrological reading of character offering the implausible suggestion that all Leos will get to the top: 'Leos always manage to emerge at the top of their particular profession, whether in design like Yves St Laurent, in business like Sir Freddy Laker or in politics like Shirley Williams and Michael Foot.' Being a Leo, it would seem from this account, is more important than anything like sex and class background, more important than educational opportunities. Being a Leo is a sign of ambition and an ability to get to the top. The sheer banality of the assessment of who gets to the top is particularly irksome coming from the magazine *Cosmopolitan*, which does sometimes investigate career prospects and the labour market.

This description of Leos characterizes another aspect of the life of heavenly bodies, namely, that they are not concerned with sexual categories. This is strange when you consider that the other commonly held assumption about essential characteristics is the belief that men and women have radically different constitutions. But it doesn't matter that there appears to be a contradiction within the ideology of given characteristics. Both the belief in the essential difference between men and women and the belief in the determination of character by birth sign serve the same function. They both feed the conviction that the character we have now is the character we were born with and that it is this character which is responsible for the kind of life we will have. Both these beliefs establish a conviction which is particularly useful for a hierarchical society. Character determines how we get on and there's not much you can do about that.

How strongly do people believe in horoscopes? Well, on one level, we read them for fun, for the momentary illusion that the story is already written, that we can plan in anticipation of the good luck that is about to befall us. But on another level, our whole society is susceptible to astrology, possibly because it represents the remnants of religious upbringing, predisposing us to the idea of something – out there in the darkened sky – plotting our fates. And for women, passivity in front of a predetermined fate is particularly recognizable. On the whole, women don't act on the world in quite the same way as men. Deprived of opportunities and limited in activities, it is small wonder that a world where things happen to you as it were by chance is not altogether implausible. And since women often feel they have little control over events, perhaps astrology offers a way of coping with this powerlessness.

But however much or little readers accept a haphazard world of chance which can be foretold, the whole of society seems to share in the underlying values expressed in horoscopes. Luck and character have become the dominant ways in which the status quo is explained and therefore justified.

Character is of course as much determined by our individual histories as it is by any anatomical or astrological attributes which might be present at birth. No doubt the new-born baby, without language and without conscious thought, is susceptible to the unspoken language of the emotions which surrounds her. But this is quite different from saying that her story is already written in the stars or in some predetermined character.

The story is accidental. Its chapters are decided by background, individual history, the opportunities open according to sex, class or race. And because the story is accidental, it could be written differently. People's fates are not destined by their characters – not unless they have been so brutalized by society that they can no longer act. In the beginning of every week lies not the possibility of a pay rise, a new acquaintance or a slice of domestic calm; there lies the possibility that we might radically change our lives.

Men's Bodies

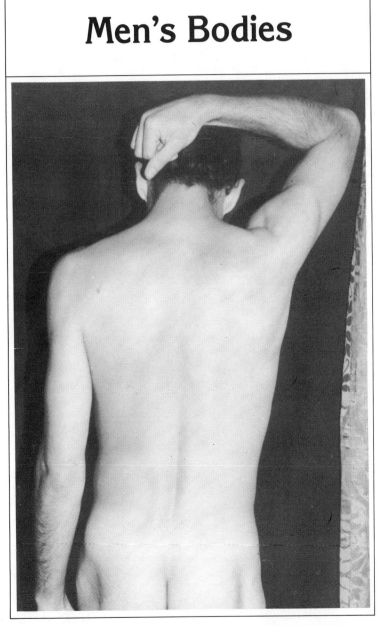

JAMES SWINSON

Absurd, stiff, different, fascinating, strange, 'feet like celery sticks and hairy bums'. These were some of the replies given when I asked about men's bodies. And not all the comments came from women! Heterosexual men defending their horror of homosexuality were insistent: of course men are attracted to women rather than men; women's bodies are so much more attractive. And even the most vigorously heterosexual women seemed to share these views, grudgingly admitting that they could understand men's 'interest' in women: after all, they said, women's bodies are much nicer.

We live in a culture which offers the body of the opposite sex as the reward at the heart of the incitement to make sexual relations. So isn't it odd that one body seems to be valued more for its curiosity value than its aesthetic appeal? Isn't this a strange contradiction at the heart of a culture which in many ways is strictly heterosexual?

The ideology which explains sexuality in our society postulates that men's bodies are designed for women, and women's bodies are designed for men. They fit together. It is a natural function and its purpose is reproduction. 'Civilization', we are told, is built on this natural basis, and pleasure was just one of the unexpected side effects. If attraction between the sexes is all so natural and straightforward, so sensible and ultimately purposeful, how is it that responses to men's bodies are characterized by the experience of strangeness, by a powerful sense of the unknown?

There has been a massive investigation of 'women the enigma', and an obsessive quest to understand women's sexuality. Our society has been saturated with images of women's bodies and representations of women's sexuality. Under this sheer weight of attention to women's bodies we seem to have become blind to something. Nobody seems to have noticed that men's bodies have quietly absented themselves. Somewhere along the line, men have managed to keep out of the glare, escaping from the relentless activity of sexual definitions. In spite of the ideology which would have us believe that women's sexuality is an enigma, it is in reality men's bodies, men's sexuality which is the true 'dark continent' of this society.[1]

The experience of the strange and the unknown seems to dominate all responses to men's bodies, be they unfavourable or

[1] Freud used this expression to describe the mystery of women's sexuality at the turn of the century.

favourable. Powerful attraction is often described in terms of an attraction to a body which is intriguingly different. Women who find men's bodies extremely attractive enjoy this experience of difference, the touch of a body which has no curves, a body which is strange and straight, solid without softness. This is the same sort of language with which women talk about penises: radically other, intriguingly different, neither soft nor hard, indefinable. Mothers too sometimes talk in the same way about their male children. Some women have described the experience of finding their sons utterly different from the outset, a difference based just on the strangeness of the body. Baby boys have bodies which do not invite identification but rather fascination for women. And sometimes it is the sort of fascination which feels shocking, so reminiscent is it of desire. Perhaps this is one of those nebulous ways in which mothers treat sons differently from daughters, in spite of every intention to treat them both in the same way.

The experience of otherness or difference, though, can easily turn against men. If a heterosexual relationship falls apart, it is not uncommon to hear women describing the discovery of an alien in their bedrooms. Of course, the disintegration of any relationship is likely to involve a distance appearing between the protagonists, a distance sometimes described as finding yourself living with a stranger. But the alien quality described by women is never simply the effect of an emotional distance. The experience is often described in vividly physical terms. Men's bodies, men's clothes, men's activities and movements suddenly appear bizarre, intrusive and utterly different. In *Original Sins*, Lisa Alther portrays the disintegration of a relationship between Jed and Sally. Sally works obsessively at remaining attractive to Jed but her discontent begins to express itself in a growing obsession with what he does with his dirty pants: 'She went round the bedroom and picked up Jed's dirty clothes, and the bath towels he'd dropped, mopped up the swamp he'd made of the bathroom floor, made their bed' (p. 371).

Implicit in this description is the growing disgust with and alienation from Jed's physical presence. In other descriptions the shock of strangeness which has turned to disgust is more forcibly described:

His red puffy face looked ridiculous against the pillow; a little smile lifted his moustache. She turned and saw him and stopped with the toothbrush half way to her mouth. She felt suddenly disgusted and outraged and shy . . . On the table by his bed lay a half-smoked pipe. His bath sponge was elbowing her as she washed; his masculine personality pervaded everything; the room reeked of it . . . Why should he lie in bed and smile? Why should he be in the bed at all – why should he be in the room at all?

Radclyffe Hall, *The Unlit Lamp*, p. 25

In both these ruined relationships, the emotions which formed the basis of attraction have died. The women look with surprise at a strange, incomprehensible presence which seems to have invaded their homes. No longer sustained by their emotional involvement in the relationship, these women suddenly view their husband's bodies in the way that this culture does generally – as strangers.

Men are physical strangers to women and to themselves because in this male-dominated society it is men who have the power to define. Men have absented themselves from the massive work currently being undertaken on sexual definitions. Men's bodies and sexuality are taken for granted, exempted from scrutiny, whereas women's bodies are extensively defined and overexposed. Sexual and social meanings are imposed on *women's* bodies, not men's. Controlling the look, men have left themselves out of the picture because a body defined is a body controlled.

Somewhere along the line, men know exactly that in rendering women the aesthetic sex they also render women the subordinate sex. This knowledge is probably unconscious but there can be no doubt about its existence. Take, for example, the reaction of heterosexual men to homosexuals. It is a common experience to hear such men saying: 'I don't care what they get up to among themselves but it disgusts me to think they might be looking at me in that way.' In what way? In the way that men regularly look at women, that is as objects of desire, desired bodies. The disgust experienced is probably a disgust based on fear, a fear that you are powerless in the light of someone's active and powerful desire. Yet on the basis of a flimsy excuse that 'it's natural', these very men are happy to sum up women in this way. Men are equally uncomfortable with male pin-ups. They sometimes become agitated in the presence of such pictures, refusing to see the bodies as attractive and reluctant to allow their own bodies to be submitted to the act of judgment that is always associated with aesthetic appreciation.

This struggle to remain in a position of dominance as the sex which defines has all sorts of consequences for the male body. Men neglect their bodies and the bodies become strange to the men themselves. This doesn't mean men are unaware of their looks;

many own up to terrible adolescent discontent with their appearances. But they also talk of sublimating that discontent. After all, they had reasoned, there's nothing a man can do to his appearance, and it doesn't really matter: men are the active, seeking sex, so it's not *men's* appearance that matters. This sublimation of self-as-desirable is one of the conditions on which male dominance rests. By refusing to see the male body as desirable, men are deemed to be doing the desiring, judging and controlling. Men's own bodies cease to be represented to themselves. But this sublimation also seems to have the effect of leaving men unconnected with their own bodies, sometimes neglectful and almost always hostile to seeing men's bodies as attractive or desirable.

One of the major consequences of men's refusal to be the desired sex, however, is that sometimes even women have difficulty in finding them attractive. There's a sort of failure of will at the heart of heterosexual desire. Perhaps it is because the neglect of aesthetic functions in relation to men's bodies has had the effect of exacerbating the differences between the sexes, of encouraging the most 'masculine' type of appearance for men's bodies. Some people might argue that it is nonsense to talk in this way. Men are men, and women are women. The sexes are different in nature and the differences are accounted for by hormones. Hormones cause hair to sprout out of the ears and down the nose and you can't blame society for that.

Actually, the *extent* of the differences in appearance between men and women varies from culture to culture and the appearance of a body can be radically influenced by the treatment it receives and the uses to which it is put. This society encourages a rigid distinction in the appearance of men and women, even though 'masculine' and 'feminine' characteristics appear on both sexes – body hair and strong muscles for instance. But if people of either sex cultivate too many characteristics of the opposite sex, they are considered peculiar. If a man manicures his nails or shaves his legs, he's likely to be mocked; a woman shaving her legs, though, is seen as expressing her natural femininity.

The most interesting aspect of this neglect of the male body, with its attendant unchecked growth of 'masculine' characteristics, is that these characteristics are rarely attractive to women. I've yet to hear a woman singing the praises of wiry hair protruding from a tightly buttoned denim shirt. And droopy moustaches and thick muscles seem rather better at provoking derision than desire. Women don't seem to be attracted to those *physical* manifestations of the extreme cultivation of masculinity. Even those women who *are* attracted to the unreconstructed masculine type admit that it's rarely the physical attributes that appeal to them; they tend to like what the body *symbolizes* rather than what it *is* – the power, protection and comfort.

Interesting, too, is the fact that unchecked masculinity *is* found attractive in one context, as a sort of parody, in male gay subculture. These characteristics are constructed as desirable in this context presumably as a sort of celebration of power which is safe as a game between people of the same sex, but entirely problematic between men and women. The physical characteristics which women actually do seem to desire in men are quite different from those suggested by the stereotype of a masculine man. For instance, sexual surprise seems to be very attractive to women, the sort of surprise associated with finding startling 'feminine' characteristics in otherwise 'masculine' appearance. Long eyelashes, pretty faces, soft hair on strong arms; all these are qualities which merge masculine and feminine attributes. Other reasons for attraction simply demonstrate a fascination with physical qualities which could just as well crop up on women: hair, skin colouring, hands, the nape of the neck. Male bottoms seem to excite similar interest – slim, trim, rounded but firm; the sort of bottom which could easily be seen on a woman.

This form of physical attraction doesn't seem to be sex-specific; it is an attraction to a particular quality or the juxtaposition of qualities. All this is a far cry from the ideologies which tell us that women are compelled towards extreme displays of masculinity. Indeed, the neglect of men's bodies has had the effect of rendering that attraction problematic. It seems possible that a primary reason for men's alienation from their own bodies is that desire between men is repressed. There can be no doubt that it is an effective mechanism in keeping men apart. In so far as men share attention to their own and each other's bodies, it is through sport and fitness routines. In this context, health and strength are erected like barriers between the desire of men. It is ironic that these devices, working to maintain heterosexuality, should introduce a pocket of turbulence into heterosexual desire. So powerful are the definitions of sexuality imposed by men that, for the whole culture, there's a problem of credibility about the attractions of men.

The Instinct

For every form of sexual arrangement approved by this society, there's an explanation in terms of natural instincts. Women tend to look after children, so there's evidence of a maternal instinct. Heterosexuality is the dominant form of sexual behaviour; that's the natural bond because animals mate. The nuclear family is the approved social unit, and the pairing and parental bond between animals proves that's natural. Instinct is the knee-jerk reflex with which this society responds to any discussion of sexual arrangements. Instinct explains why we do what we do. Instinct also explains why we shouldn't do what some people do – an elastic concept.

Instinct is a term which seems to be particularly useful for explaining away conventional forms of 'male' and 'female' behaviour. Instinct explains male aggression and instinct explains female passivity and the desire to nurture others. One rationale of instinct dominates all these ideas about male and female behaviour, parenting and so on. This is the rationale of reproduction, and it runs thus: the central purpose of human life is to reproduce itself but men and women have different relations to this aim, and this explains the difference between male and female behaviour. Men would do it with whomever and whatever, strewing their seed around as widely as possible, in the hope that some will hit home. This makes men naturally promiscuous and naturally aggressive, competing as they do with other men. Women, however, are more fussy; women select their partners either as good providers or as good genetic stock, and then set about securing these partners. Once trapped in marriage, however, men acquire a taste for it, and especially a commitment to their offspring.

But when it comes to it, just how useful are these arguments about natural instincts – so prevalent, so plastic, so unexplained? At one level, such arguments are very comforting. After all, if the way you are living is 'natural', you can feel better about it. However difficult things may be in your life, you can explain it all away. 'It's natural. It can't be helped.' But however comforting, these ideas obscure more than they explain. Take the defence of male aggression, where the term instinct is used to explain the curious enmeshing of violence and sex which sometimes characterizes some aspects of male sexuality in this society.

In 1977, Mr Nicholas Fairburn, who was then Solicitor General for Scotland, described rape as 'a crime which I have never been forced to commit'. He went on, 'MPs would do well to remember that rape involves an activity which is normal. It is part of the business of men and women that they hunt and be hunted and say "yes" and "no" and mean the opposite. If it is misinterpreted let a jury decide whether it was reasonable to misinterpret it' (quoted in the *Guardian*, 22 January 1982). Natural behaviour here is a world of male predators, aggressive animals who hunt the female of the species. The female is passive and coy; at first she will say no but secretly she may want the advances to continue – how else could she have her desires and stay 'modest'? So by this rationale rape is merely a normal pursuit of sex where sometimes the female signals are misread. Fairburn's definition of normal sex might well be rape with consent. The usual legal definition of rape is the opposite: rape is sex without consent. Both views share certain assumptions about sexual relations: men's role in sex is to initiate and (sometimes) to wait for permission to proceed. Women's role is to give the go-ahead or withhold it.

The idea that female sexuality works as a lure and a response to male predatory and probing sexuality is quite patently an ideology belonging to a particular historical epoch. The ideology has the effect of endorsing the mixture of violence and sex which characterizes some aspects of masculine behaviour in contemporary society. And the ideology also endorses a definite view of female passivity: women's sexuality is limited to making a choice between yes and no. In some areas of the media we can see such views actively promoted. For instance, in some forms of tabloid journalism, it is customary to refer to women as 'birds' or sex kittens (usually a reference which goes beside a 'topless' picture). Men, however, accrue such epithets as 'the office wolf'. And those 'sex offenders', in whom such newspapers are excessively interested, are referred to as 'monsters' and 'fiends': 'A savage sex monster was being hunted last night after raping an eight-year-old girl inside her school' (*Sun*, 22 May 1981). Such language promotes a view of the sexes as two species; the strong species – dogs and wolves – pursue the weak – birds and kittens. When the customary limits are overstepped, men become monsters, gone too far in their natural pursuits.

There is in fact nothing in nature which permits a reading of male aggression as inevitable, female passivity and weakness as eternal. Certainly, animals mate, animals breed and animals sometimes fight (often male animals, but not always). But it is an illegitimate leap of thought to deduce that the same *meanings* can be derived from the same acts in both the human and animal worlds.

There can be no way in which aggression, dominance, mating and so on have the same place within human society as they do in animal society. There are crucial differences between human and animal societies; in human societies divisions between the sexes and between groups have enmeshed with specifically *human* history, where dominance and power are closely associated with the control of resources and therefore imply that other members of society are placed in 'subordinate' and weak positions.

As far as can be deduced, animals have not yet instituted a division of labour geared towards the production of surplus resources for the future. As a result, there's no evidence that certain groups either create or appropriate a surplus of resources and then control the distribution of these resources for future profit. Indeed, as far as the evidence goes, immediate survival is the name of the game. Complex societies, complex ecologies exist, but food is consumed as it appears or at most stored for the ensuing winter. As far as we know, when squirrels bury acorns, they do not have in mind harvesting from the resulting trees in twenty years' time, and selling acorns at vastly inflated prices to the hedgehogs.

Some human societies, though not all, do just this.[1] Food and goods are produced and accumulated not to ensure immediate survival but to be used for exchange for other goods. And in some societies, this process of exchange is linked to the creation of profit – profit from the control of surplus goods and resources. In these societies, the creation of profit has also developed linked to unequal distribution of the resources: one group controls how the surplus is distributed, and in short has power over other groups.

In animal society there's a startling absence of complex accumulation and unequal distribution of resources. Of course, scientists, not to be daunted by the shocking absence of bourgeois traits among animals, have found what they regard as a solution. 'Genes', they say, are every animal's natural property. Thus all mating, parenting and territorial behaviour is seen as a sort of economic calculation for the future. Both animals and humans share this common concern – to perpetuate their genes.

Whatever animals are up to when they mate, it is ridiculous to

---

[1] Not all societies create a surplus which is then distributed inequitably. Certain societies produce surplus resources which are then distributed equitably between the whole society.

establish a logical connection between the activities of the selfish gene and a complex society where control of the surplus produces certain groups in dominance and others in positions of inferiority.[2] Genes can go on for ever without a bean in their pocket. But in some human societies, the activity of reproduction has been harnessed to the control of property. In some hierarchical societies, property is appropriated and controlled, and transmitted to the future via biological families, thus ensuring the reproduction of inequalities in the future. In such societies, women's reproductive capacities are linked to one particular family. Thus some hierarchies are based on reproductive relationship (kinship relations or what we call family relations); certain groups appropriate and control the surplus to their own advantage, and against the interests of other members of that society.

The history of this process of accumulation is none other than the specific history of *property* relations. In some cases, like our own, it has led to the capitalist mode of production. This history of property relations is not the same as territoriality, mating and male aggression. The history of property relations belongs to human history not as an inevitable aspect of humanity but as a chance by-product whose outcome has been the inequitable control of resources. Now in the animal world some animals do suffer or get destroyed – a harsh winter might wipe out the wren population; one species may find its access to a watering hole limited by the aggression of another; there may be a shortage of food due to natural failure. But as far as anyone can tell animals do not have an inequitable distribution of available resources within species, or a system of biological reproduction ensuring that the inequitable distribution as well as the genes continue in perpetuity.

Now the point of this argument is to demonstrate that aggression, dominance and power in our society do not occur as in nature. They occur in a society based on divisions and on divisions which have overwhelming consequences for what a person's position in that society will be. Among others, the division between men and women has fatal consequences for the *social* position of those sexes. For in the end, men and women do have an unequal relation to the distribution of resources. The issue has been horrendously confused because virtually all political arguments – from the left and the right alike – insist on seeing men and women as one. We are led to believe that

2 See Richard Dawkins, *The Selfish Gene*, Paladin, 1978.

because men and women marry, they therefore make up one family, with identical access to social resources. But the truth is that, whatever the class, men and women do have a different relation to social resources. Because of inequalities in the job market, because of how care for children and the elderly is arranged, and because of the way the state treats women, women rarely have the same relation to resources as men. And in a hierarchical society, this separation of groups from the control of resources is not a neutral event. Groups separated from the means of production are viewed as inferior by those in control. We're not in the same situation as animals. Male animals may fight; dominant males may sit on their dung heaps. But it is illegitimate to assume that the female of the species is therefore 'inferior', 'weaker', 'subordinate'. Indeed, this whole language of inferiority, weakness, subordination, dominance and power is a *human* language. It arises from certain societies where some groups have been disadvantaged to the benefit of others.

In human society, sexuality has become entangled in this separation of groups into 'privileged', 'dominant' and 'disadvantaged' or 'weak'. Because the relations between the sexes are unequal, sexual relations are imbued with meanings about dominance and subordination. What we encounter in rape, then, has nothing to do with the rituals of mating according to seasonal patterns, as in the animal world. It may well be a ritual but it is a ritual connected more with symbolic statements than with seasonal activities. As far as the evidence goes, rape seems to be tied up with the assertion of power – that's why it is always difficult to draw a distinction between violence against women, sexual violence and violently imposed sexual intercourse (rape). Quite often, they have the same meanings – the humiliation of one group. When men feel compelled to act aggressively towards women, they may well be driven by the internal psychic expression of external circumstances. Ideologies lead men to believe that women are inferior, yet that women are desirable. Ideologies also tell men (as they told Nicholas Fairburn) that normal sex means men take the initiative. It isn't altogether surprising, given the prevalence of such beliefs, that rape should appear in this society as a way of satisfying both the desire to dominate and the desire to have sex.

Far from being a natural expression of male and female sexual behaviour, male aggression is more likely to be the ritualistic enactment of cultural meanings about sex. And this is true of just about every manifestation of sexual activity. Sex in human society is never instinctual; sex is always an activity wrapped in cultural meanings, cultural prescriptions, and cultural constraints.

Even the 'normal' pairing of men and women – apparently the most natural of human activities – is infused with cultural meanings. Of course men and women have sex, but 'mating and reproduction' neither exhausts the kinds of sexual activity which are possible and enjoyable, nor does it tell us anything about the variety of meanings attached to 'doing it' by different cultures or indeed individuals. Indeed, only by distorting or ignoring the evidence do some people assert the universality and naturalness of the marriage bond. Mrs Thatcher's adviser on the family concluded his book on the subject with a rhetorical flourish, aimed at proving the naturalness of the married bond: 'Marriage and the family make other experiences, both pleasant and unpleasant, seem a little tame and bloodless. And it is difficult to resist the conclusion that a way of living which is both so intense and so enduring must somehow come naturally to us, that it is part of being human' (Ferdinand Mount, *The Subversive Family*).

Such rhetorical appeals about the enduring bond of the natural family are useful only as ways of avoiding serious scholarship on the subject of sex and the family. They characterize the manipulation of the question of sex and the family for political ends, where material is selected and distorted according to overall political aims. There are impressive distortions at work which can represent a narrow bond between men and women as the universal and natural, instinctual form.

To make this assertion rounds all humans up into one happy family, the animal family. But to do so shows a breathtaking disregard first for the diversity of family life within our own culture, and secondly for the different meanings attached to marriage in other cultures.[3]

Only in our culture, for instance, is the bond between a man and a woman expected to provide all emotional and material support. In other cultures, a marriage ceremony may well be far more important for the relationship which it creates between the kin of the man and woman rather than for the bond itself. The heterosexual bond tends

---

[3] For a useful summary of the kinds of families currently living in Britain see, *Families in the Future* from the Study Commission on the Family, 1983. This document makes it clear that the 'typical' family is not typical, that Britain has a diversity of 'household forms' – single parents, elderly people on their own, and different ethnic family forms.

to be the basis for the alliances between groups, presumably because this bond implies procreation and most societies are interested in this. But the implications of this bond are by no means the same from culture to culture, nor is the strictness with which it is enforced.

Even that biological act – reproduction – which seems so unavoidable, so enduring, is a biological act which may be interpreted differently according to cultures and different individuals. Women's natural instinct for reproduction, the maternal instinct, is supposed to be the base line of all her behaviour, her ultimate *raison d'être*. Indeed, arguments about the natural instinct seem to reach a climax around the designation of women as the reproductive sex, and therefore the caring and nurturing sex. It is clear that women's anatomy makes her the childbearing sex; it is clear also that most women experience extraordinarily powerful feelings towards their children. But it is also clear that the notion of the reproductive instinct has again acted as a barrier to understanding sexual relations, rather than as a source of illumination.

There seems to be an enormous problem about the conventional designation of women as the reproductive sex. The fact that women's bodies are geared up for reproduction is taken as the fundamental explanation for women's sexual behaviour. These natural phenomena are supposed to explain everything about women – why we stay at home, why we don't get promoted, why we don't get well paid, why we cook and clean. But when it comes to sexuality, which sex really is the reproductive sex? Men or women? When it comes to *sexuality*, men not women are the reproductive sex. There are only about four days in a month when sex with men might result in conception for women. For the rest of the time, women are capable of a multiple orgasmic sexuality which – in theory at least – produces nothing but pleasure. Even on a fertile day, women's orgasm is not tied to reproduction. A woman could conceive without orgasm; sexual pleasure is irrelevant to the reproductive function. Men's sexuality on the other hand is unavoidably reproductive. Men can't even masturbate without some visible evidence of their reproductive capacity. Orgasm and reproduction are truly synonymous for men.

I can't help but suspect a case of projection here. Women are labelled the reproductive sex and stigmatized thus by society. Designated the reproductive sex, we also become the sex which has to assume the full responsibility for reproduction. Women must take responsibility for contraception; women must also take primary responsibility for child care – all because of our reproductive sexuality. But the equation made between women's ability to give birth, women's sexual behaviour and women's responsibility for child care is not a necessary equation, derived from nature. The equation has emerged through the history of this society and has been projected on to nature.

Recent changes in the position of women have allowed the apparently indissoluble link between women and reproduction to become at least slightly attenuated. Widespread contraception is one change, but general shifts in attitude and sexual practice are probably more important. Both have allowed heterosexual women to be explicit about a sexuality autonomous from reproduction, an autonomy which previously was only possible for lesbians. For those with children, or wanting children, or for those who want to forgo the experience, it is now much easier to talk in terms of what children mean or will mean in their lives.

Instead of a blanket term – the maternal instinct – dumped over the whole area of childbirth, childbirth can now be explored as a biological event the meaning of which is very different for different individuals, and the consequences of which are enormous.

'Don't ever believe anyone if they say having children won't change your life. It does. I'm not saying I regretted having children but some of it is very difficult. It's the problem of having people totally dependent on you, who are always around, dying for you to be interested in them, involving you in their quarrels, following you to the toilet, never giving you a moment's peace. In some ways, I don't think I'm a very good mother in the conventional sense – my husband's a lot more maternal.' 'Having children is all the joy and the problems of suddenly having another person in your life, whose own survival depends on your every move.' 'I get on quite well with children but I just can't imagine having one of my own. I can't imagine disrupting my life like that.' 'It's been very difficult to combine a career with children, I've had to make sacrifices. Once you've been away from work for a bit, your man's career begins to take precedence. We had exactly the same qualifications from college – that's where we met. Now I'm moving where his job takes him and trying to fit in. In fact I haven't been able to find a job. There's not much work here and, you know, in spite of all they say, employers aren't keen on women with young children. I'm very happy with my children. I love them. In many ways, it's much more rewarding than paid work. But sometimes I despair. I feel as if I've lost touch with the world.' 'I just don't want children. I'm put off by what that relationship of dependency does to you. I've seen too many people screwed up by awful relationships with their parents – so much guilt and obligation. I want to have other kinds of loving relationships'.

Even the positive, overwhelming desire to have children isn't a uniform desire. There are so many different *reasons* why women want children:

'I had not longed for children, thought about the subject much or discussed it with my partner. A very indulged cat was the only evidence that the maternal instinct might be waiting to take the world by surprise. There is no doubt that some instinct took over and was sufficiently strong to overcome the grave doubts I had about life with children ... In retrospect I also wanted to repay my parents for all they gave me as a child – the only way to do this seemed to be to give to my own children in some way.' 'I still feel little natural attraction towards other people's children, but am obviously deeply involved with my own. I simply obeyed an instinct by having them, and they (not the lifestyle they have dictated!) have exceeded my expectation.'

That instinct or urge to have children seems to have so many different explanations: some speak of a sense that a child might fill up a feeling of loneliness, some of a sensual desire for a child's body close to their own, some of a desire just to have the experience, some of a desire for a 'normal' family, some of a sense that having children has just got to be better than being pushed around in rotten low-paid jobs, and some of the desire to have a particular person's child. All these different *meanings* are often referred to as an instinct. But the variety of reasons and consequences and the variety of circumstances in which a child could be born are a sure indication that the same anatomical events may have vastly different meanings in the lives of individuals. The differences between the desires and consequences surrounding pregnancy are like a microcosm of the differences between cultures. There are no simple, unilateral interpretations of biological acts.

People have bodies, anatomies, and certain anatomical capacities. But our bodies are not our destinies. Around the sensations of the body, the activities of reproduction and sex, are a whole series of complicated emotions and meanings. Some come from general cultural definitions of sexuality, but some come from our own personal histories. If humans are animals, it isn't stretching credibility to insist that humans are also natural, therefore anything they do is natural. Things are natural because they happen to us, but beyond that, there are drastic differences between how societies organize them, what they mean in our lives and how we feel about those events.

And Desire . . .

Unto the woman God said, 'I will greatly multiply thy sorrow and thy conception; in sorrow thou shalt bring forth children; and thy desire shall be to thy husband and he shall rule over thee.'

THE BIBLE

The phenomenology that emerges from the analytic experience is certainly of a kind to demonstrate in desire the paradoxical, deviant, erratic, eccentric, even scandalous character by which [desire] is distinguished from need. This fact has been too often affirmed not to have been obvious to moralists worthy of the name.

JACQUES LACAN

. . . women cannot *exist*: the category of woman is by definition that which does not fit into *existence*. So women's activity can only be negative, in opposition to what currently exists, saying 'that's not right' and 'there's something more'. I mean by 'woman' what is not represented, what remains unspoken, what is left out of namings and ideologies.

JULIA KRISTEVA

From the moment I see you, I can no longer speak; but my tongue breaks, and under my skin, suddenly slides a subtle fire: my eyes are without sight, my ears buzz, sweat trickles down my body, a thrill seizes me all over; I grow greener than the grass, and, very nearly, I feel myself dying.

SAPPHO

We may believe we fuck stripped of social artifice; in bed, we even feel we touch the bedrock of human nature itself. But we are deceived, flesh is not an irreducible human universal. Although the erotic relationship may seem to exist freely, on its own terms, among the distorted social relationships of the bourgeois society, it is, in fact, the most self-conscious of all human relationships, a direct confrontation of two beings whose actions in the bed are wholly determined by their acts when they are out of it . . . Flesh comes to us out of history; so does the repression and taboo that governs our experience of flesh.

ANGELA CARTER

Do we *truly* need a *true* sex? With a persistence that borders on stubbornness, modern Western societies have answered in the affirmative. They have obstinately brought into play this question of a 'true sex' in an order of things where one might have imagined that all that counted was the reality of the body and the intensity of its pleasures.

MICHEL FOUCAULT

It is essential to understand clearly that the concepts of 'masculine' and 'feminine', whose meaning seems so unambiguous to ordinary people, are among the most confused that occur in science ... observation shows that in human beings pure masculinity and femininity is not to be found either in a psychological or biological sense. Every individual on the contrary displays a mixture of the character traits belonging to his own and to the opposite sex and he shows a combination of activity and passivity whether or not these last character traits tally with his biological ones.

SIGMUND FREUD

When jealous, I suffer four times over: because I'm jealous, because I reproach myself for being jealous, because I'm afraid my jealousy doesn't affect the person I'm jealous of, because I'm being carried away by a cliché: I suffer by being excluded, by being aggressive, by being mad, and by being banal.

ROLAND BARTHES

Man has one sexuality to match his one organ. But woman does not. She has two sexual organs at least, which are not identifiable separately. She has many others as well. Her sexuality is always at least double, and is really plural. How does our culture want to see it? How is it written about? How is it misrepresented?

Well, women's pleasure isn't a choice between clitoral activity and vaginal passivity for example. The pleasure of a vaginal caress isn't the same as a clitoral caress. They converge in the female orgasm in an irreplaceable way. Breasts being caressed, the vulva being touched, the lips half opened, the to-and-fro of pressure on the back wall of the vagina, the light touch at the neck of the womb, etc. This only evokes a few of the more specifically feminine pleasures. All are neglected in the normal way of considering sexual difference – or how it isn't considered. For 'the other sex' is usually seen merely as indispensable complement of the male organ.

LUCE IRIGARY

You fit into me
Like a hook into an eye
A fish hook,
An open eye
MARGARET ATTWOOD

Further Reading

Apart from a small number of articles, I have limited suggestions for further reading to a small number of easily-available books. There are, however, a number of journals or regular publications which deal with some of the issues covered by this book.

These publications are:

Screen, the journal for the Society for Education in Film & Television, 29 Old Compton Street, London WIV 5PL
Feminist Review, 65 Manor Road, London N16
Spare Rib, 27 Clerkenwell Close, London ECIR OAT
Working Papers in Cultural Studies, The Centre for Contemporary Cultural Studies, University of Birmingham, Birmingham 15

Images

Barthes, R. *Mythologies*, Paladin 1973
Barthes, R. *Camera Lucida – Reflections on Photography*, Cape 1981
Berger, J. *Ways of Seeing*, Penguin 1972
British Film Institute, *Selling Pictures* (BFI Education Image Project)
Cherniz, K. *Womansize*, The Women's Press 1983
Freud, S. *On Narcissism: An Introduction*, Standard Edition, Vol II
Lurie, A. *The Language of Clothes*, Heinemann 1981
Orbach, S. *Fat is a Feminist Issue*, Hamlyn 1979
Williamson, J. *Decoding Advertisements*, Boyars 1978
Wilson, E. *What is to be Done about Violence against Women?*, Penguin 1983

The Media

Film and Television

The British Film Institute have produced several useful monographs analysing visual imagery, eg:

Brundson, C. and Morley, D. *Everyday TV: Nationwide*, 1978
Dyer et al, *Coronation Street*, BFI 1978
Kaplan, E. *Women in Film Noir*
More generally, there are:
Bordwell, D. & Thompson, K. *Film Art*, Addison Wesley 1980
Ellis, J. *Visible Fictions*, Routledge & Kegan Paul 1982

Women's Magazines

McRobbie, A. *Jackie*, Centre for Contemporary Cultural Studies,
    Stencilled Paper 1977
White, C. *Women's Magazines*, Hutchinson 1970
Winship, J. 'Sexuality for Sale' in *Culture, Media, Language* (op. cit.)

Radio

Local Radio Workship, *Local Radio in London*
Moss & Higgins, *Sounds Real*, University of Queensland 1982
Karpf, A. 'Women and Radio' in *Women's Studies International Quar-
    terly*, 1980 vol 3.

Narrative/Fantasy

Barthes, R. *S/Z*, Cape 1976
Belsey, C. *Critical Practice*, Methuen 1980
Ellis, J. *Visible Fictions*, Routledge & Kegan Paul 1982
Freud, S. *The Family Romance*, Standard Edition, vol IX
Freud, S. *Creative Writers and Day Dreaming*, Standard Edition, vol II
Heath, S. *Questions of Cinema*, Macmillan 1981
ed. Reis, J. & Lemon, L. T. *Russian Formalist Criticism*, University
    of Nebraska 1972
Silverstone, R. *The Message of Television Myth and Narrative in Contem-
    porary Culture*, Heinemann 1978

Language

Black, M. & Coward, R. 'Linguistic, Social and Sexual Relations',
    in *Screen Education*, Summer 1981, no 39
Coward, R. & Ellis, J. *Language and Materialism*, Routledge &
    Kegan Paul 1977
Miller, K. & Swift, R. *Women and Words*, Penguin 1979
Spender, D. *Man-made Language*, Routledge & Kegan Paul 1980

Women's Position in the Family and Employment

Barrett, M. *Women's Oppression Today*, Verso Books, 1980
Cook, A. & Campbell, B. *Sweet Freedom*, Picador 1982
ed. Segal, L. *What is to be done about the Family?*, Penguin 1983
The Study Commission on the Family, *Families in the Future*, 1983

The History of Sexuality

Foucault, M. *The History of Sexuality*, Allen Lane 1979
Heath, S. *The Sexual Fix*, Macmillan 1982
Rowbotham, S. *Hidden from History*, Pluto Press 1974
Rowbotham, S. *Women's Consciousness, Man's World*, Penguin 1976
Weeks, J. *Sex, Politics and Society*, Longman 1981

Psychoanalytic Accounts of Sexuality

Freud, S. *Standard Edition*, The International Library of Psycho-
    analysis, Hogarth Press (see especially, *On Sexuality*, Penguin
    Freud Library 1977)
Klein, M. *Contributions to Psychoanalysis*, Hogarth Press 1950
Lacan, J. *Ecrits*, Tavistock 1977
Lacan, J. *Four Fundamental Concepts of Psychoanalysis*, Penguin 1980
Mitchell, J. *Psychoanalysis and Feminism*, Allen Lane 1976

Selected Grove Press Paperbacks

17650-2 OE, KENZABURO / A Personal Matter / $6.95
17002-4 OE, KENZABURO / Teach Us To Outgrow Our Madness / $4.95

17242-6 PAZ, OCTAVIO / The Labyrinth of Solitude / $9.95
17084-9 PINTER, HAROLD / Betrayal / $3.95
17232-9 PINTER, HAROLD / The Birthday Party & The Room / $6.95
17251-5 PINTER, HAROLD / The Homecoming / $5.95
17761-4 PINTER, HAROLD / Old Times / $6.95
17827-0 RAHULA, WALPOLA / What the Buddha Taught / $6.95
17658-8 REAGE, PAULINE / Story of O, Part II: Return to the Chateau / $3.95
62169-7 RECHY, JOHN / City of Night / $4.50
62171-9 RECHY, JOHN / Numbers / $8.95
17983-8 ROBBE-GRILLET, ALAIN / Djinn / $4.95
17117-9 ROBBE-GRILLET, ALAIN / The Voyeur / $4.95
62498-X ROSSET, PETER and VANDERMEER, JOHN / The Nicaragua Reader / $8.95
17446-1 RULFO, JUAN / Pedro Paramo / $3.95
17119-5 SADE, MARQUIS DE / The 120 Days of Sodom and Other Writings / $12.50
62009-7 SEGALL, J. PETER / Deduct This Book: How Not to Pay Taxes While Ronald Reagan is President / $6.95
17467-4 SELBY, HUBERT / Last Exit to Brooklyn / $2.95
62040-2 SETO, JUDITH ROBERTS / The Young Actor's Workbook / $8.95
17948-X SHAWN, WALLACE, and GREGORY, ANDRE / My Dinner with Andre / $5.95
17887-4 SINGH, KHUSHWANT / Train to Pakistan / $3.25
17797-5 SNOW, EDGAR / Red Star Over China / $9.95
17939-0 SRI NISARGADATTA MAHARAJ / Seeds of Consciousness / $9.95
17260-4 STOPPARD, TOM / Rosencrantz and Guildenstern Are Dead / $3.95
17884-X STOPPARD, TOM / Travesties / $3.95
17474-7 SUZUKI, D. T. / Introduction to Zen Buddhism / $3.95
17599-9 THELWELL, MICHAEL / The Harder They Come: A Novel about Jamaica / $7.95
17969-2 TOOLE, JOHN KENNEDY / A Confederacy of Dunces / $4.50
62168-9 TUTUOLA, AMOS / The Palm-Wine Drinkard / $4.50
62189-1 UNGERER, TOMI / Far Out Isn't Far Enough (Illus.) / $12.95
17211-6 WALEY, ARTHUR / Monkey / $8.95
17418-6 WATTS, ALAN W. / The Spirit of Zen / $3.95

GROVE PRESS, INC., 196 West Houston St., New York, N.Y. 10014